MYSTERY OF THE IRISH WILDERNESS
DOMINIC MORAN
BORN
in Ireland
D1596096

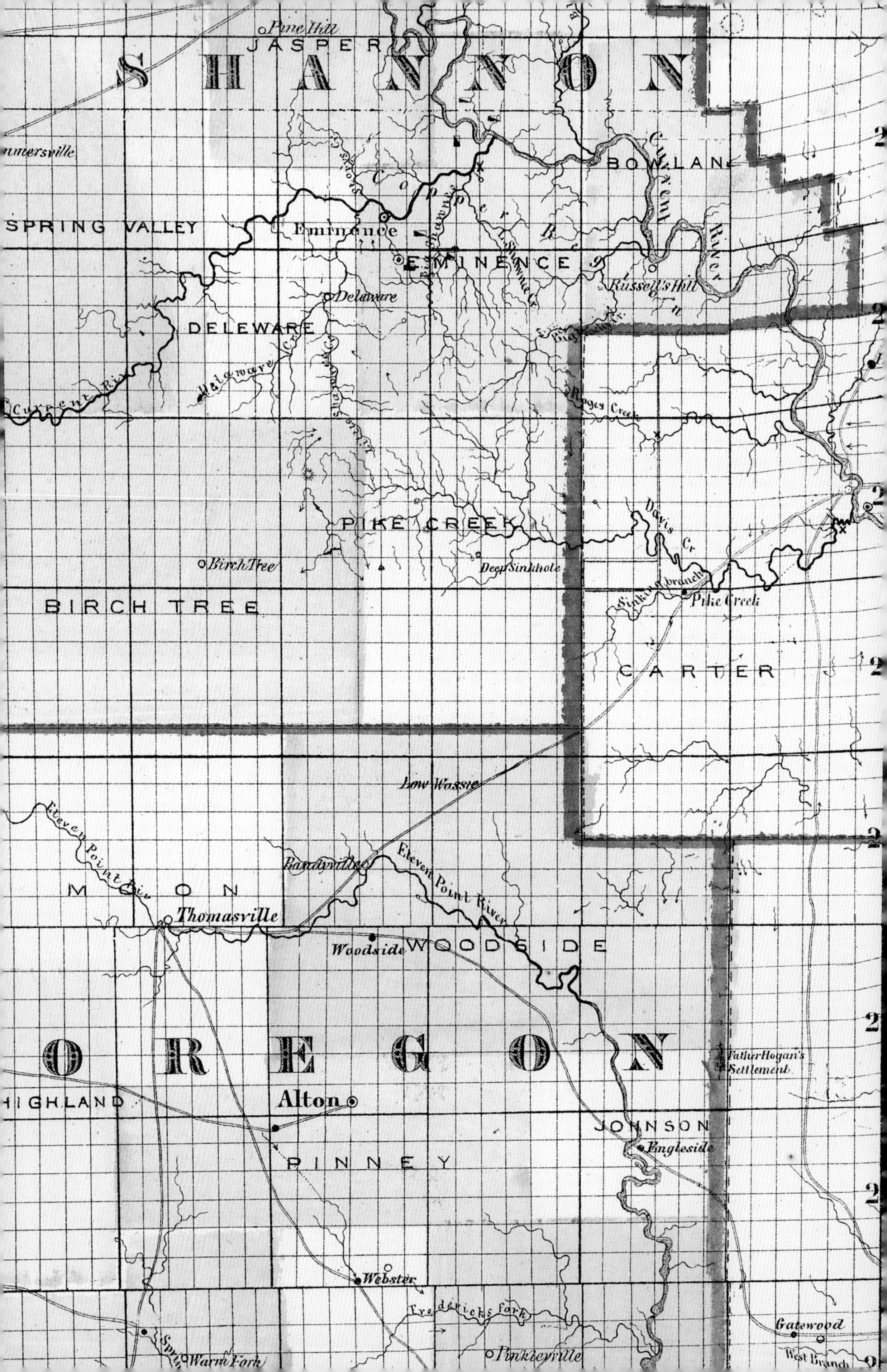

Pine Hill
JASPER
SHANNON
BOWLAN
SPRING VALLEY
Emmence
EMINENCE
Copper Cr
Current River
Russell's Hill
Delaware
DELEWARE
Delaware Cr
Current Riv
Rogers Creek
PIKE CREEK
Birch Tree
Deep Sinkhole
Davis Cr
Sinking branch
Pike Creek
BIRCH TREE
CARTER
Low Wassie
Eleven Point River
Eleven Point Riv
MON
Thomasville
Woodside
WOODSIDE
OREGON
Father Hogan's Settlement
HIGHLAND
Alton
JOHNSON
Engleside
PINNEY
Webster
Fredericks fork
Warm Fork
Gatewood
West Branch

MAC
977.88
P347

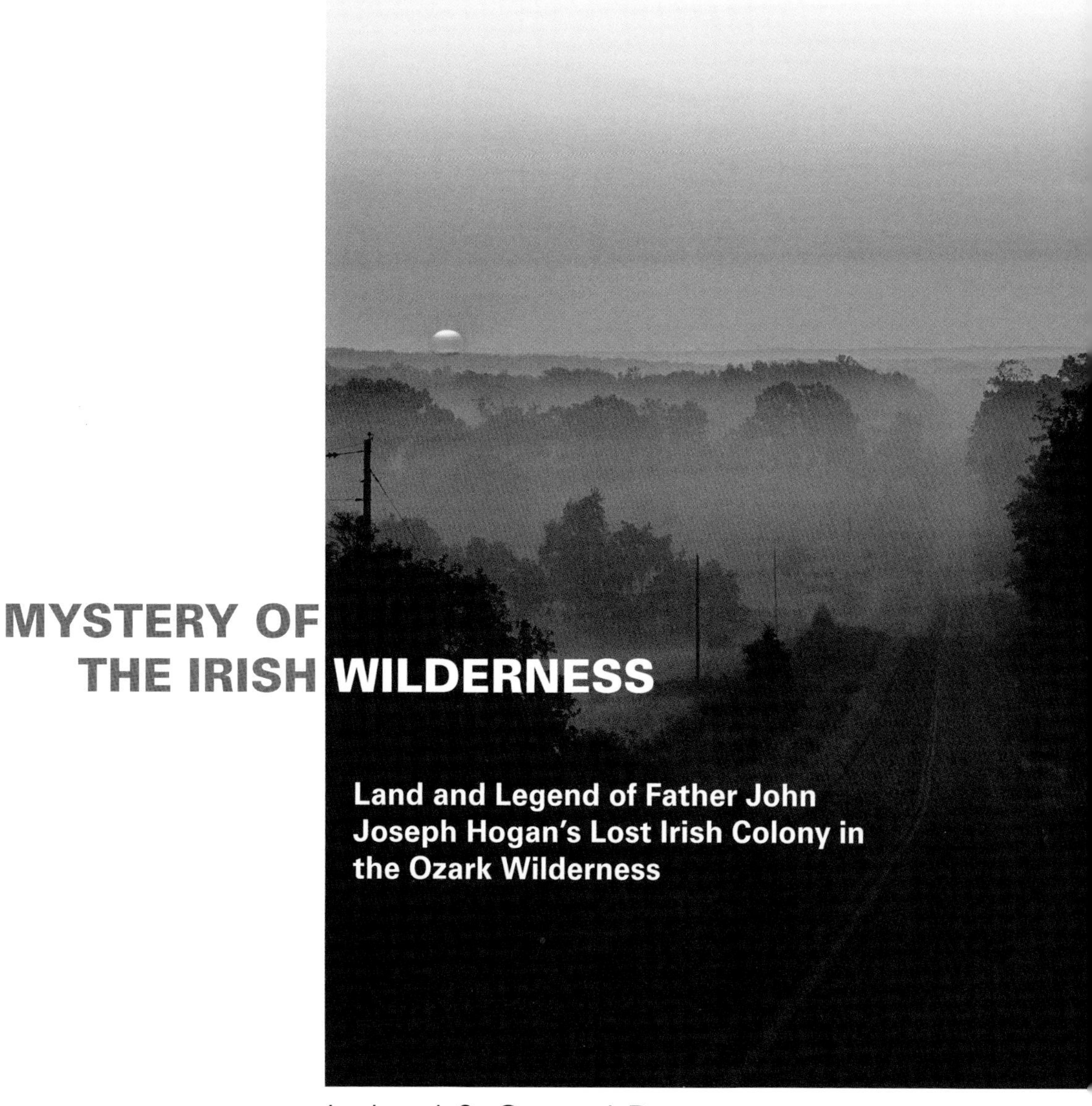

MYSTERY OF THE IRISH WILDERNESS

Land and Legend of Father John Joseph Hogan's Lost Irish Colony in the Ozark Wilderness

Leland & Crystal Payton

Missouri Center for the Book

Missouri Authors Collection

Lens & Pen Press

Dedicated to all Irish-American priests who, like Father Hogan, have contributed to our democratic traditions.

Text and photographs © 2008
Leland & Crystal Payton

First edition.

All rights reserved.

Library of Congress Control Number: 2008920152

ISBN 978-0-9673925-4-7

prepress by Ross Payton,
Slang Design
rpayton@gmail.com

manufactured in Singapore

Lens & Pen Press
Springfield, Missouri

lensandpen@yahoo.com

visit the Lens & Pen Web site
www.beautifulozarks.com

Cover: Greer Springs.
Page 1: Ponder Cemetery.
Page 2: Campbell's 1875 map of Missouri showing the correct location of Father Hogan's settlement.
Page 3: View across the Eleven Point River.
Back Cover: Sign to Irish Wilderness, 160 Highway.

PREFACE & ACKNOWLEDGEMENTS

Being familiar with both the Ozarks and north Missouri and their citizenry, Father J.J. Hogan's book, *On the Mission in Missouri*, has long had special resonance for us. When Rev. C. Michael Coleman, archivist for the Kansas City-St. Joseph Diocese guided us to the file cabinet of Hogan's papers we learned the pioneer priest himself was an intriguing subject. Audrey P. Newcomer, director of the St. Louis Archdiocese archives, thrilled us when she provided a small file of papers that contained a notebook that Father Hogan had carried in a saddlebag when he was founding the Irish colony. These Catholic archives documents have contained many revelations. Interpretations of them are solely ours.

We thank also the librarians of Local History and Genealogy at Springfield-Greene County Library; the Special Collection and Archives, Duane G. Meyers Library, Missouri State University; the Miller Nichols Library Special Collections, University of Missouri-Kansas City; and the Western Historical Manuscript Collection at Rolla, Missouri. Aldo Leopold authority, Dr. Susan Flader, of the University of Missouri-Columbia, provided a copy of Leopold's letter.

Cynthia Price, U. S. Forest Service Archaeologist and Mike Jones, river guide, were helpful. All the floaters, farmers and feds we met in Oregon and Ripley counties were friendly and outgoing. We encountered no bushwhackers driving the lonely back roads of the Irish Wilderness.

We continue to be influenced by the democratic esthetic of John Margolies' books. Our friends, Rollie and Bettina Sparrowe, are examples that there is a continuing interest in seeking a realistic balance between the interests of man and of nature. Our son, Ross Payton, not only did all the prepress work, he also helped proofread the manuscript. In the somewhat unlikely event there is demand for a Japanese edition we will be calling on his brother, Strader, for translation.

CONTENTS

IRISH WILDERNESS ACT OF 1984

Throughout most of American history the duly elected members of Congress have sold, even given away, hundreds of millions of acres of public lands to encourage development. Originally, the United States was land-rich with a sparse coastal population of mostly poor people. Friend of the small farmer, Thomas Jefferson, and capitalist advocate, Alexander Hamilton, fought over how to manage the public domain. Both favored the conversion of raw land into taxable assets. The only question was if the rapid conversion of wilderness to wealth would be best accomplished by populist or by elitist ownership and exploitation. Their argument was how best to achieve these materialistic goals.

In the 1960s some legislation, like that era's arts and fashion, departed from tradition. Such an anomalous piece of legislation is the Wilderness Preservation Act signed into law by President Lyndon Johnson on September 3, 1964. Even the typical dry legalese of its prose does not disguise its anti-technological, Thoreau-ian philosophy. Both Jefferson and Hamilton would have puzzled over the idea that Congress should mandate the identification and protection of "undeveloped federal lands retaining its primitive character and influence, without permanent improvements or human habitation." Romanticism was not in flower in the early days of our republic, so such notions were not widespread. Those wishing to find solitude in the wilderness of eighteenth century America certainly didn't need federal assistance. Nature in the era of our founding fathers was the subject of scientific study or inspiration for art, not a source of moral values or habitat for leisure.

From the initial designation of nine million acres, the Act

IRISH
WILDERNESS
MARK TWAIN
National
Forest

now protects over one hundred million acres. Although the largest "untrammeled" acreages of public land were out west or in Alaska, groups who enjoyed recreating in the wilds effectively lobbied to stretch the language of the Wilderness Act to include places that were in a primitive but not pristine natural state.

Along the east bank of the Eleven Point River in Oregon County, Missouri was a large holding of second growth U.S. Forest Service land. Government wildlife biologists had valued its isolation and relative roadlessness since the 1930s. Including part of The Irish, as it was called, in the wilderness system became a priority among Missouri preservationists. It was a controversial proposal. Sierra Club members from St. Louis were pitted against folks from the nearby hamlet of Wilderness on the issue of including a substantial tract along the Eleven Point River in the wilderness system. Many of the locals worked the timber for a living. Rural Ozarkers are generally disdainful of government controls, even though many rely on government employment or benefits. With the help of select politicians, the urban preservationists won:

> *Be it enacted by the Senate and House of Representatives of the United States of America in Congress assembled,* That this

Four miles northwest of the site of Hogan's church is Wilderness—a dozen houses, a Protestant church, a closed country store and a WPA-era school, now a community center. Certainly, it was within the region locally called the Irish Wilderness. Conceivably, when the store obtained a post office in the 1880s, the name was shortened.

> Act may be cited as the "Irish Wilderness Act of 1984". Sec, 2, (a) In furtherance of the purposes of the Wilderness Act (16 U.S.C. 1131-1136), certain lands in the Mark Twain National Forest, Missouri, which comprise approximately sixteen thousand five hundred acres, as generally depicted on a map entitled "Irish Wilderness", dated March 27, 1984, are hereby designated as wilderness and shall be known as the Irish Wilderness.

If you wish to see this place you must walk or ride a horse. Wilderness regulations prohibit motor vehicles or mountain bikes. Be forewarned—it's easy to get turned around in the hills and hollows near the river. A compass and map are mandatory.

In the hip pocket of most backpackers is a U.S. Forest Service fold-up map that delineates in a thin red line an 18.6 mile trail through the congressionally designated wilderness. Under "Welcome to The Irish Wilderness" is a short explanation of the name:

> In the mid 1800s a Catholic priest, Father John Hogan of St. Louis had a dream of a place where Irish immigrants could escape the oppression of urban life in St. Louis. It was in this wild area of the Missouri Ozarks that Father Hogan said people could "so profoundly worship as in the depth of that leafy forest...where solitude and the heart of man united in praise and wonder of the Great Creator."
>
> The timing of the ill-fated settlement however was not right, as the Civil War erupted. The Irish Wilderness was caught in the middle, became a "no man's land" and was raided by both Union and Confederate troops as well as bushwhackers. It is not certain what happened to Father Hogan's Irish immigrants, but after the war they were gone.
>
> The mystery of the Irish immigrants is part of the character of the land today. Since that time the area has been logged and grazed clean of vegetation. But today, because of the efforts of the Civilian Conservation Corps, the Forest Service, and the amazing ability of the land, the Irish Wilderness again has regained the same character that Father Hogan found.

The specialty of the United States Forest Service is land management, not history. Eddie Bauer-clad backpackers have dreams of a place to "escape the oppression of urban life" not Potato Famine immigrants. Union troops alone harassed the Irish settlers, not Confederate.

The idea that Smoky and the Civilian Conservation Corps have restored the area to "the same character that Father Hogan found" is a bit of a stretch. Long gone are the vast pineries, grassy barrens, and monster burr oaks that grew in the bottoms. Another part of the publication acknowledges that "a few old growth stands remain but the majority of trees are less than 50 years old." Government foresters know their trees. The brochure writer just added a little old-time conservation mythos left over from the F.D.R. era.

Objections aside, the observation that "the mystery of the Irish immigrants is part of the character of the land today" couldn't be a better summary. What happened long ago in these remote Ozark hills remains unclear. Records are few and multiple interpretations abound. In spite of the lack of

Riders at the Camp Five Trailhead prepare for a day trip around the 18.6 mile loop through the official Irish Wilderness. Hikers are advised in the U. S. Forest Service pamphlet to allow two days for this journey and "if you become lost don't panic." Though the trail is fairly well marked and the area is crisscrossed by old logging roads, the Irish preserve is 16,500 acres of disorienting, densely forested hills and hollows.

hard documentation (or perhaps because of it), the Irish settlement has become the stuff of legend and a subject matter for generations of feature writers. It's an event commemorated in the language of an act of Congress.

But the brief history should have mentioned that the Irish colony was spread over parts of four, conceivably five, counties. The official 16,500 acre preserve is but a small part of a much bigger territory the Irish attempted to settle.

Welcome to this larger Irish Wilderness. Don't get lost.

FATHER HOGAN'S MISSION

In June of 1857, Father John Joseph Hogan was, after his repeated requests, relieved of his duties at St. Michael's Parish by St. Louis Archbishop Peter Kenrick and allowed "an opportunity to go into the interior of North Missouri where there was no priest, and there build a chapel or two as nucleuses of congregations." Growing up in a village near Limerick, Ireland, Hogan had "taken great delight reading the *Annals of the Society for the Propagation of the Faith.*" Now 28, he could live his dream of "braving all obstacles" to advance the Christian faith far from home. Most of Hogan's 1892 book, *On the Mission in Missouri, 1857-1868,* unfolds on the newly settled prairies. Intertwined with his missionary efforts north of the Missouri River however is the only firsthand account of the Irish colony in the wooded wilds of southern Missouri. His book vividly portrays the animated times just before, during and after the War Between the States. Sharply observed and objective in tone, passages like this that address John Hogan's past or motivation are rare:

Hogan knew the fertile tall grass prairies of northern Missouri would be better farmland than the forested, rocky Ozarks. In the late 1850s, accessible prairie lands were sold or had been given to the railroads as an incentive. The only big tracts of cheap government land lay in southern Missouri.

> What I have to say for myself is stated cumulatively in what I have hereinbefore said on the abnormal condition of Catholic emigrants in Missouri and on the remedy to better that condition. If I would advance some of many other reasons, they would be the following. In early boyhood I took great delight reading in the *Annals of the Society for the Propagation of the Faith*, the achievements of Missionary Priests in far off countries, braving all obstacles to convert benighted nations to the light of Christianity. I followed these Holy Missionaries in spirit and with all the ardor of my soul into China, Japan, Borneo, Siam, Tongking, and other equally remote or unknown regions

> of the world. But nowhere did their lives and labors seem so grand and heroic to me as on the Great Plains of North America, along the sources and banks of the world famed rivers, the Missouri and the Mississippi and their numerous tributaries—a country which they enrapturously described as of surpassing beauty, as fresh as if new made from the hand of the Creator, and inhabited only by wild men, who shared their illimitable solitude with countless wild animals, which they pursued with all the ardor of the chase over grassy hunting grounds.

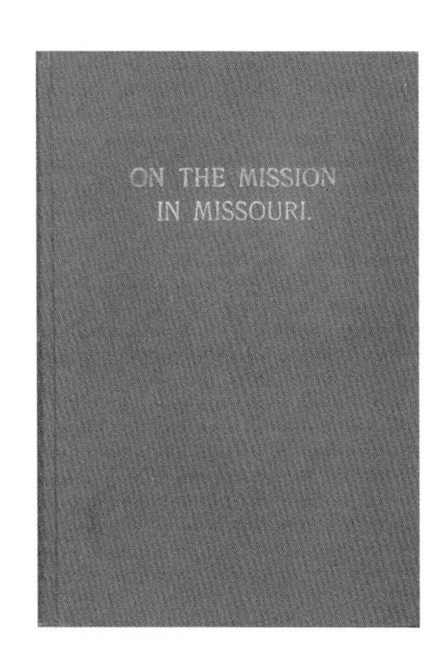

Decades after the Irish colony vanished, John Joseph Hogan wrote a book on his days as a pioneer priest. *On The Mission In Missouri*, published in 1892, reveals Father Hogan to have been a resourceful traveler and a keen observer with a wry sense of humor. His straightforward prose captured the energy and enthusiasm of the frontier, as well as its hardship and tragedy. His description of Missouri before the plow and axe transformed the native prairie and virgin forests is poignant. If not for Father Hogan's account, the story of the Irish Wilderness might have vanished with the fading of local folklore.

Riding a horse named John the Baptist by its former owner, a Baptist minister, Hogan found the country north of the Missouri River nearly "as fresh as if new made from the hand of the Creator." At that date, vast tracts of native prairie had not been plowed. "Wild men" who shared "illimitable solitude with countless wild animals" had disappeared long before. Instead, he found camps of wild Irish railroad workers who were not sharing their solitude with good Catholic girls:

> During the years 1854-55 on the mission at St. John's church, St. Louis, I observed that the Catholic servant girls attending that church, were not less than three hundred or more...The Catholic young men, likewise for the most part emigrants from Ireland, not finding work in the cities, and there being no work for them on farms in competition with slave labor, were obliged to seek employment on the railroads, and to live in camps and move from place to place, as the shifting nature of their employment required. The total separation of these emigrants, one party not finding employment where the other did, was in a most anomalous condition, resulting in practically debarring them from intermarriage, and from marriage of whatever sort.

On his foray into north Missouri, Hogan found the prairie country exhilarating. He had even located a few unserved Catholics settlers. A lot in Chillicothe had been donated for a church. But the larger problem of creating and keeping together families of newly emigrated Irish had not been solved:

> So far my main purpose in setting out from St. Louis, to find a place where Catholics might settle on land, was not advanced any. My inquiries, wherever I had traveled through

> North Missouri, led to the information that the Government land in that region of country had all been sold, or given away to railroads, and that the present owners held it at high price; about twenty dollars an acre for improved land, and for unimproved land about ten dollars an acre, which sum absolutely prohibited purchase by poor people, such as Catholic emigrants mostly were.

A page later under the heading "The Remedy," Father Hogan revealed his plan that would lead to the ambitious settlement of Potato Famine Irish in the Ozark wilderness:

> It seemed to me to be my duty to do whatever might be in my power, to aid these people to rise from their condition of servitude, to ownership and cultivation of land, so as to secure for them, beyond doubt, a settled and permanent mode of existence that would accord better with their higher social aspirations and religious principles. This, however, could not be done in North Missouri, where land was held at too high a price. I had heard that there were still remaining unsold large tracts of government land in southern Missouri, that could be bought for one dollar an acre, and some of it for a less price; and that it was of a moderate fertility, though much inferior to the land in North Missouri. One dollar an acre seemed to me, to be within the possible reach of comparatively poor people. Having procured from the district land office at Jackson, Cape Girardeau county, Missouri, plots and surveys of wide tracts of vacant government lands in the said region of country, I lost no time setting out and journeying to see these lands.

If Hogan writes little about himself in *On the Mission in Missouri,* something of the character of the priest who has decided to look for vacant government land in the Ozarks is revealed in his accounts of traveling north Missouri.

> On this journey (to Clinton and Caldwell counties), I proceeded by easy stages on horseback, as John the Baptist was weighted down, less by the rider than the large satchel and saddlebags, containing vestments, chalice, missal, altar-stone, and other necessaries for the mission. Crossing Grind Stone Creek, a tributary of Grand River, flowing in a northerly direction, in the southeast part of De Kalb county, at about mid-day, the weather being warm, I permitted John, my namesake, to wade in past knee deep, and dropping the bridle

> loose on his neck, I let him stoop down to drink. Having drunk to his content, delighted with the clear, cool water, he sat down leisurely, leaning over on one side and keeping his head above water. I went over too, endeavoring all the while, to keep my head, as the horse did, above water. We were both in the Jordan. I hastened to get out of it. He seemed in no hurry to finish the ceremony. The whole occurrence was so ludicrous, and the Baptist evidently so well up to it, that my sides shook with laughter. As the weather was dry and the sun bright and warm, the books and vestments, spread out on the grassy prairie, soon regained their former good condition. The poor missionary, however, very meekly submitted to the drying process, his raiment remaining on his back. Soon, all put to rights again, I was once more on the move, endeavoring to reach the hamlet of Mirabile before nightfall, the place being then fully fifteen miles distant.

After humorously coping with being dunked in Grindstone Creek, his temporary joy at finding a group of Catholics in Mirabile is dampened by the words of a prosperous businessman:

> "Reverend Father, we are happy to welcome you here, and to have the opportunity to hear Mass and receive the Sacraments. We have deemed it best that this be done, not in an open and public manner, but privately amongst ourselves, and within the precincts of our dwellings. There is much prejudice here to us as Catholics and against our Church, and this prejudice, if aroused by any public ceremony or display on our part, may be taken as a challenge and in very bad spirit by our non-Catholic friends. It is better, as I think, for these reasons, and because there are so few of us here, and our means very limited, that the building of a church be not thought of at present." The other Catholics who stood by, listening, expressed opinions agreeing with his. There was no hope of building a church at Mirabile.

Throughout the book, John Hogan describes his mounts in detail, suggesting he had a country upbringing. Indeed, in a small book, *Fifty Years Ago: A Memoir,* published in 1907, his recollections of life in rural Ireland explain his competence at adroitly dealing with life on the rough and ready American frontier:

> Riding was one of our favorite sports in those days. We

usually indulged in it on school holidays, or when the master was sick, which meant we were scott-free until he had got over the measles. Our riding-course comprised two large adjoining fields, called Barnhill and Feahmoor, which were traversed by lines of hillocks with sharp ascents and declivities and by steep earthen dikes or ramparts curtained by water. This was the topography of Feahmoor, where the riding exploits took place. The Barnhill was rather more rocky, and therefore more suggestive of cracked skulls and broken bones of inexpert young jockies. These fields, to the great delight of us youngsters, had a never-failing supply of lively, well-fed donkeys, young and old. Old donkeys were not boys' first choice, on account of their vicious habits, of biting their riders legs and rushing their riders against thorny hedges and stone walls. Young donkeys were more choice, as more inexperienced in warfare with bad boys, who usually wished to enjoy a ride without being put hors de combat. To ride a fast young donkey and to hold on his back trotting and galloping and in spite of hoisting, kicking, and rearing, constituted a boy an undergraduate in assmanship. But the honor of a diploma was reserved for the final test, to be made with the rider's face towards the donkey's tail. At this tournament, it was against the rules, and was inconvenient besides, to use a bridle; but the rider might hold on to the wool as best he could. Success achieved under these circumstances was proclaimed by the whole field with vociferous rejoicing. Discomfiture, on the other hand, never failed to be followed by roars of side-splitting laughter, especially if the young knight-errant should happen to land heels up in a mud-puddle or in a ditch of water. Not every boy, after a defeat or two of that kind, would be willing to try it again; and boys with soiled jackets and pants and muddied shirt-tuckers were usually not gallant enough to face their mammas at home, for full well they knew what strong faith these mammas had in the virtue of the tough birch twig that was kept ready for use and that was well seasoned.

Our less exciting exercises were fishing, swimming, hurling, running, leaping, vaulting, wrestling, throwing cast, climbing trees, playing leap-frog, scaling old castles and old abbey walls. In all these accomplishments I was post-graduate at the ripe age of ten.

Though there was scattered hostility to his faith, he didn't encounter the institutional persecution of Catholicism in the New World as had been done by the English in his native land. Prejudice, Hogan believed, would be dissipated if the American public were better informed. The lone mounted priest capitalized on the novelty he presented in the yet barely churched, de facto Protestant country:

> When it became known that there was a priest in town, great was the curiosity to see him. It was supposed he should be an elderly man, of grave, austere appearance. Some who had seen him, said he was a young man and by no means austere. Strangers, young and old, who entered the town, were eyed closely as they passed by. Some averred that a showman, entering town, clad in fine raiment, and riding a dappled white and bay horse, was mistaken for the priest. The priest, however, could not long keep himself within the cloud. When he came to be known, he was found to be a tall thin man, wearing plain black travel-stained clothes; and his horse was not a dappled prancing steed, but a plain little sorrel pacer. The next craze was to see the priest in his vestments and to hear what he had to say. As there was no Catholic church in town, the surmises were various, as to which of the Protestant churches he would exhibit himself in.
>
> The non-Catholics, however, took care that he should get none of their churches, and they were not without having been asked, but not by the priest, for the favor. Ed. Darlington, editor of an able and very independent little paper then published at Chillicothe, had much to say of the preachers, and in no very complimentary strain, on the subject of their refusal. And to show them that the priest did not stand in need of their churches, he got the use of the Court House, and had it cleaned and fitted up for the priest to lecture in. He, moreover, attended the priest's lectures, and liberally advertised them free of charge. At the close of the lectures, which were continued every evening for a week, John Graves, the oldest citizen and the first settler in the town, donated a lot to the priest to build a church on. The lot was surveyed and staked out by George H. Nettleton, the eminent citizen and great railroad president and manager, then a young man of prepossessing manners, appearance and address, a division engineer on the construction of the Hannibal and St. Joseph railroad, and for the moment engaged in laying out John Graves' urban farm into streets and town lots.

The down-to-earth style of priest Hogan did not clash with the pragmatism and Jacksonian democratic spirit

Americans first settled along the big rivers of Missouri. River towns like Jefferson City were well served by steamboats. Railroads were just beginning to provide transportation as Father Hogan began his missions to the interior. Going to the prairies of north Missouri and the deep Ozarks required extensive stagecoach, buckboard or horseback travel.

of early Missourians. Community leaders would listen to his lectures and were impressed with his directness and his commitment to his faith. Some who would help him establish churches were not even Catholic.

Archbishop of St. Louis, Peter Richard Kenrick, sanctioned these risky missions, but the project was Father Hogan's choice and responsibility.

> His Grace called on me, at St. Michael's church, my former home, where I was staying for the time being. "I would not think," he said, "of sending you out to North Missouri, on that mission. But since you are willing to undertake it, you may do so in God's name. I give you these light missionary vestments, with portable chalice and altar-stone. They are from my own private chapel. I hope you will succeed in your undertaking. But if you ever wish to return to the city I will give you your parish back, or one as good in place of it."

Fellow clergymen were less reticent in expressing fear for Hogan's safety. In the subchapter, "Friendship's Pleading," Hogan relates their misgivings:

> But there were difficulties yet in the way. They came from dear friends who regarded the undertaking as visionary. A devoted priest, a particular friend of mine, insisted on holding out against me to the last. Shouldering me back at every street corner on the way to the railroad depot, he almost violently resisted me getting on the cars. I got aboard the train however, and was soon on my way from the Fourteenth Street depot in St. Louis to Jefferson City, the western terminus at that time of the Missouri Pacific Railway. From Jefferson City I went by steamboat to Brunswick.

On Father Hogan's first exploratory trip, he returned to St. Louis on the packet Spread Eagle. It was not only swarms of mosquitoes that kept him awake that hot night on the Missouri River:

> The darkies of whom there were about fifty on board, all athletic men, suffered many cruel hardships. Their keepers, a few armed men, held them chained together in squads, so as to hinder them from getting away at landing places. At night, formed into line, shoulder to shoulder, their faces turned one

way, manacled with iron handcuffs man to man, they were made to lie down on their backs, on the boiler deck of the boat, without pillow, mattress, or covering–a position they could not change for one instant during the whole night, not even so much as to lie on one side. The groans of the poor fellows, as they clanked their manacled hands against the deck, or dragged and slashed in pain their booted heels on the rough boards on which they lay, were truly heart-rending. They were accused of no crime, were torn away without a minute's notice from their homes, husbands separated from wives and children, sons separated from parents, brothers and sisters. All were forced to leave dear friends and loved scenes behind them. Love of money caused it all. Traders had bought them and were taking them to trade them again, and for a much higher price, in the slave marts of St. Louis and New Orleans.

Seven years before, when a student of the Theological Seminary of St. Louis, the task was given me to write an essay on liberty, which, like all such essays, was to be read and criticized before the rhetoric class. My subject led me to make some comments on negro slavery, and somewhat in the strain of Thomas Moore and Daniel O'Connell on the same subject. "Young man," said the Professor to me, "I have nothing to say to you on the merit of your essay, but this: when you go on the mission, if you give expression to sentiments such as these, you will be driven from home decorated with a coat of tar and feathers, and fortunate you will be, if nothing worse befall you."

Though scarcely a radical, John Joseph Hogan had dangerous views on slavery in a slave state. His temperament and background enabled him to cope with the rude circumstances of the frontier. However, the ensuing political and social chaos of a civil war would threaten the success of his missions, especially the remote southern colony.

Johnson's Shut-ins, in the St. Francois Mountains, was within a 150-square-mile land grant made to Father James Maxwell by the Spanish crown in 1799. Maxwell had proposed importing a large group of destitute Irish to save them from "British tyranny and persecution to which they were exposed on account of their religion." Nothing came of Father Maxwell's colony. When Father Hogan passed through this rugged area he noted its poor soil and pushed on. There is no indication he was aware of this earlier scheme to populate the Ozarks with Irish settlers.

JOURNEYING IN SOUTHERN MISSOURI

Father Hogan's missionary success in north Missouri was minimal at first, but he had become adept at frontier travel. Hogan met small adversities with good humor. Having to share a shack with hogs and getting doused when his horse lay down in a muddy river, he thought amusing. The tall young Irishman engaged in backwoods-style Socratic debates about the merits of Catholicism with settlers who had never seen a priest.

He had little money but was skilled at borrowing horses or wheedling railroad passes. Using a combination of trains, steamboats and stagecoaches, he could usually get close enough to his destination for a day's ride across the unbroken prairie. Hogan's Irish country upbringing (his father had been a farmer and a cattle dealer) made him an experienced horseman. But riding the Ozark frontier was different:

Fog masks a tourist hotel beyond the Highway 60 bridge at Van Buren. Father Hogan forded the Current River here on his first exploratory trip. The forests and wildlife have changed, but the valleys are still deep and the hillsides steep. Ozark rivers rise dramatically after a heavy rain and subside quickly, as Hogan noted a century and a half ago.

> Traveling in Southern Missouri was even more difficult than in Northern Missouri, and was for the most part possible only on horseback, on account of the ruggedness of the country and the rockiness of the roads. The rivers, being shallow and hard-bedded, did not require bridges, as fords were numerous and good. Occasionally, in heavy rains, the rivers rose quickly past fording; but as they subsided as quickly, the delay to let the high water run by was not long. The difficulties arose mostly from the long distances to be traversed along trackless divides or over deep valleys and steep hill-sides through the forests.

The itinerary he listed in his book of his first trip southward is short. It would have been an arduous journey. Chillicothe and the "trackless divide" between the Eleven Point River

By 1857, the alluvial bottoms along even secondary streams like Pike Creek were occupied by settlers. Hogan was shopping for land in a region in which the best agricultural land had been taken.

and the Current River, where he and the surveyor searched for suitable land, are 400 miles apart—even on today's highways. Deep in the Ozarks, he often followed winding trails inherited from the Indians:

> Traveling by way of Brunswick, Jefferson City, St. Louis, Old Mines, Potosi, Iron Mountain and Frederick Town, I halted at Greenville, in Wayne County, where I hired a surveyor familiar with the country. I examined the lands on the head waters of Little Black River, Cane Creek, Brushy Creek, in Ripley (now Carter) county, and entered four hundred and eighty acres in a body on Ten Mile Creek, making arrangements at once to put men thereon, opening and cultivating it. With the surveyor I rode westward, across the Current River, by Van Buren, up Pike Creek, thence southward over the great divide east of Eleven Points River as far as the head waters of Buffalo Creek, thence eastward along Buffalo Creek and its tributaries to a ford on Current River. At this place there was a mill and homestead owned and occupied by a man named Appollinaris Tucker; he and his family were the only Catholics known to be residing at that time in that district. At the time of my arrival, Mrs. Tucker was in the last stages of her mortal illness, in which it seemed God's Holy Will that she should linger until her longings could be gratified to receive the last Sacraments;

Appollinaris and Ellen Tucker purchased government land in 1854 and 1856 in Ripley County, Missouri. Presumably, Ellen was Mrs. Tucker, to whom Father Hogan administered the Last Rites on his first trip in 1857. There is no record of the mill after the Civil War or what became of Appollinaris. Tucker Bay Spring, large (24 million gallons a day) but curiously unstudied, flows into the Current River.

and, as it happened, from the hands, of the first priest known to have come into that region of country. After Mrs. Tucker's death, I returned homewards, by way of Iron Mountain, St. Louis, and Hannibal, to Chillicothe.

John Joseph Hogan's first assignment as a priest was St. Joachim's church at Old Mines, Missouri in 1852-53. Lead and tiff had been mined in the area since the early 1700s. Although most of the miners were French, the mission here was founded by the Irish priest James Maxwell in 1814.

In the cemetery of St. Joachim's Church in Old Mines is the grave of Father John James McCaffrey who drowned in the Meramec River in 1836. He was answering a sick call when he fell from his horse and was swept down river. Evidently not all missionary priests were skilled, experienced horsemen like Hogan as equestrian injury and fatalities were not uncommon.

Another Irishman, James Fox, was pastor when Hogan was assigned.

In the late 1850s, track was being laid just east of Old Mines by the St. Louis and Iron Mountain Railroad. Fox likely visited the camps of the Irish workers and probably felt dismayed at their conditions. Hogan passed through Old Mines on his way south and may have visited Fox. At any rate, he wrote his friend upon his return to north Missouri:

> Arrived at Chillicothe, I corresponded without delay, with my dear friend and worthy brother priest, Rev. James Fox, rector of St. Joachim's church, Old Mines, Missouri, who as I well knew, was deeply concerned for the matter of land ownership

St. Joachim's Church in Old Mines, Missouri, was consecrated in 1831. Although renovated several times, the grace of its Palladian-style architecture has not been lost. The churches Father Hogan built in Chillicothe and in the Ozark wilderness would not be so distinguished.

and occupancy by Catholic emigrants. The incidents of my late journey, which I related to him, so interested him that he requested to be permitted to accompany me on another such journey, if I should have occasion to make one. I wrote to him to be ready and that I would soon call on him.

Before many days, and in the latter part of November, we set out together on horseback from Old Mines. Traveling by way of Caledonia and Edgehill, we passed through Centerville the county seat of Reynolds County. Thence entering Shannon County, we descended Blair Creek, remarkable for its alternate lime-stone and red porphyry hills. Afterwards, we crossed the Current River at the mouth of Jack's Fork, thence to Eminence, thence to Birch Tree, thence to Thomasville, thence to Pike

Mining justified an early railroad from St. Louis into the St. Francois Mountains. This wood engraving from an 1857 *Ballou's Pictorial* published in Boston shows Ironton, the terminus of the railroad until after the Civil War. Workers on this line were called "the Iron Mountain Irish." There is speculation Hogan recruited some of them for his colony, but he doesn't mention it.

> Creek, thence to Van Buren, thence to Ten Mile Creek, thence to Black River, thence by way of Otter Creek, McKenzie Creek and Big Creek, through Caledonia and Potosi, homeward.
>
> Reynolds County we found entirely unfit for settlement, not one tenth of the land being tillable. Shannon and Oregon counties had much tillable land, perhaps one-third of the whole area, but none of it of prime quality except the river alluvial bottoms. Everywhere through these two last named counties, there was good stock range and abundance of valuable pine forest

Back in northwest Missouri Father Hogan continued as before, seeking and visiting Catholic settlers and railroad camps. In January of 1858 he traveled south again. On this trip he is accompanied by Father Walsh, who like Hogan, was a native of County Limerick, Ireland:

> REV. William Walsh, the devoted zealous pastor of St. Peter's

On Hogan's second trip to the Ozarks in late November, 1857, he was accompanied by Father James Fox. They forded the Current River on horseback at this spot where the Current's principal tributary, the Jacks Fork River, enters.

> church, Jefferson City, ever a loving faithful friend of the emigrant, took the greatest possible interest in every effort made to lead the good Catholic Irish people from the railroad shanties and the back streets and cellars of the cities, to locate them on lands.

Crossing the Black River in freezing weather on horseback Walsh got his boots and clothing wet and caught pneumonia. While Father Walsh recuperated in a "poor uncomfortable tavern in Greenville," Hogan traveled to the Jackson Government Land Office where he employed an agent to transact business for the settlers. He returned to Greenville, found Walsh "in much better health and courage".

> We again set out together and rode by easy stages towards the Iron Mountain and Potosi, thence homeward by rail to St. Louis; he going to Jefferson City and I to Chillicothe.

LAND FOR PEOPLE OF SMALL MEANS

Over many primitive trails Father John Joseph Hogan had ridden looking for suitable land for a colony of poor Irish immigrants. His appraisal of the hilly, forested Ozark wilderness was realistic, but cautiously optimistic:

> The information we had gathered was, that Ripley, Oregon and Howell counties afforded good advantages for settlement to people of small means and of patient, frugal, industrious habits. The country as we found, was quite healthy. Land was cheap. The land was by no means all good, but enough of it was good to support many inhabitants, if not a dense population. About one-third of the whole area could be tilled for orchards, vineyards, or the usual vegetable or cereal crops; and the yield was far more generous than the appearance of the soil would indicate. The ground, too, when once broken and cleared, was easily cultivated. There was plenty of timber of good quality everywhere at hand, that made it an easy task to build dwellings, barns, stables, fences, and to furnish fuel. Springs and streams of pure, clear water were abundant except in a few localities. The lands that could not be cultivated were fairly grassy and could feed many cattle. The price of government land was from twelve and a half cents to one dollar and twenty five cents per acre. The best cultivated lands, of which there were many farms along the rivers and streams, with houses, stables, barns and fences, could be bought for ten dollars an acre, buildings and improvements included. Some could be bought for five and some even for three dollars an acre. These prices were much lower than for unimproved land in North Missouri. The winters, too, were longer and severer in northern Missouri than in southern Missouri. Likewise, the scarcity or total want of timber for fuel, fencing and building purposes, made it impossible for a poor man, or

This now-closed road in the National Forest Irish Wilderness unit is a mile west of the site of Father Hogan's log church. It goes to the Eleven Point River and may be one of the trails that existed during the time of the Irish settlement.

> for a man not comparatively wealthy, to acquire and improve land in North Missouri. All things considered, there was no reason whatever to doubt, that emigrants who could not own land in their native countries, however much they desired to do so, and who as renters maintained themselves there even on small patches of barren land, could by using the same thrift and energy in southern Missouri, successfully cultivate land, and establish on it for themselves and their posterity a permanent homestead.

While the land "was by no means all good" Hogan concluded the region could support a modest settlement. Unlike the rich, but treeless prairies of north Missouri there was an abundance of timber to build housing and fences and for firewood. Soils developed under bottomland forests were rich, at least initially. The frequent fires set by Indians and continued by pioneers created "barrens"—savannah-like

A relic water mill and log cabin at Falling Springs within the Mark Twain National Forest in Oregon County. When Father Hogan located his colony in this region there were only scattered pioneer homesteads. The great migration west had bypassed the rougher Ozarks for better land.

openings in the oak forests. Livestock could be set loose in this open range to graze the prairie grass.

Best of all most of this land could be bought at the U.S. Government Land Offices in 40 to 320 acre units for 12 1/2 cents an acre. Forty dollars for half a square mile of land was cheap, even in the mid-nineteenth century.

It wasn't only Hogan and his Irish colonists who were taking advantage of this bargain. Locals bought land. Under the Preemption Act of 1852 squatters were allowed to buy property they were living on but didn't have title to. The Graduation Act of 1854 made that land affordable. Speculators and would-be pioneers from all over the United States took a flyer on Ozark land in the late 1850s.

Selling public lands was an important source of revenue for the federal government. However, settlement of the frontier affected the economy of each region of the country differently. Laws regulating land sales were fiercely debated in Congress. Northeastern manufacturing interests feared the drain on their labor force if land were priced so low it induced westward migration. Frontier states naturally favored cheap land and easy terms. With the rise of

Isaac Kelly is thought to be the first American pioneer on the Current River. In 1824, he purchased land he had earlier settled within this fertile bend of the Current River (seen here uncharacteristically muddy after a rain). Thirty-five years later, Hogan's Irish immigrants purchased tracts in the rocky hills across the river. Although little government land sold before the big price reduction in 1854, few good farm sites were left by the late 1850s.

Jacksonian democracy some aspects of federal land sale policies became more favorable to settlers. But until Senator Thomas Hart Benton of Missouri finally got his Graduation Act passed by Congress in 1854 all public land carried a per-acre price tag of $1.25. Good farming and commercial properties had been snapped up for that figure. Marginal lands, like the Ozarks, were largely passed over.

The Graduation Act reduced the price of land depending on the time it had been offered to the public. Land unsold for twenty-five to thirty years was now reduced from $1.25 to 25 cents an acre. Most of the land Hogan had looked at had been on the market for over thirty years and went to the rock bottom price of 12 1/2 cents an acre

This drastic price reduction created a land rush. In the area that is now Carter County, only thirty land titles were filed before the Graduation Act. In the 1850s, 1,021 claims were registered. Surveyors, government officials and land agents were overwhelmed by the flood of applications. The drastic price reduction had the desired effect in encouraging settlement. Hogan described the chaos:

The 1808 Kelly Cemetery is in a bend in the Current River opposite Kelly Bluff. Kelly is an Irish, not a typical Scotch-Irish, name. This would seem to confirm Hogan's observation that there had been some settlers from southern Ireland in the region.

As matters went, people from the eastern and middle states, as well as Missourians, had their agents and surveyors selecting and applying for land; and many made land entries at random and without any attempt at selection or examination. In the rush for land, applicants upon entering their names on the books of the land office, with the description of the land wanted, had often to wait months for their turn to come following the hundreds before them. Usually, too, the information long waited for, was disappointing; the land asked for, and that was vacant when the application was made, having been reached sooner by persons more forward on the lists. From this cause the surveyors' work and charges were often lost, at the expense of the applicant, and sometimes thrice over in succession, the cost increasing with each disappointment. Soon, to gratify the wishes of applicants, and because nothing better could be done, entries of some kind of land were made, and hundreds of applications were returned, no land whatever having been entered. The following extracts from letters of the agent for the colony, near the land office, give some idea of the difficulties that existed.

JACKSON, Mo., APRIL 15, 1858.
The South West 1/4 Section 7, and the North West 1/4 of

On his first trip Hogan looked at land on the small tributaries of the Black River. He thought the gentle valleys of streams like Ten Mile Creek had agricultural promise—as this photograph confirms. Unfortunately, his claims in this region fell through and his colony was forced to locate deeper in the wilderness.

the North West 1/4 Section 12, Township 26 North, Range 3 East, embraced in Maurice O'Brien's application, was sold in February last. A wrong marking of the plats showed the above tracts vacant. The South 1/2 Section 1, Township 26 North; Range 2 East, embraced in James Evans' application, has also been sold. You will please furnish other tracts in lieu of the above.
Very respectfully, G. W. FERGUSON.

JACKSON, Mo., APRIL 30, 1858.
I find from examination that the following tracts, applied for by you, have been sold, to-wit; application of James Murray, North West 1/4, and lot I North East 1/4, Section 6; application of Denis Sullivan, South West 1/4, Section 21; application of Denis Hurley, South West 1/4 Section 24, application of Thomas Mulvehille, South East 1/4, Section 22; application of Michael Mara, North 1/2, Section 22; application of Stephen McNamara, West 1/2, Section 23; application of Patrick Griffin, South 1/2 of North East 1/4, Section 36; application of Patrick Rowe, North West 1/4, Section 30. All these have been sold to others.
Very respectfully, G. W. FERGUSON.

At this stage the land entry business was turned over entirely

When Hogan rode through, this unusually broad valley of the Eleven Point River surrounding Thomasville, it would have been planted in corn, not pasture grasses as it is today. The county seat was Thomasville when Father Hogan first rode through the region looking for land but moved to the more centrally located town of Alton in 1859.

> to A. & D. O'Brien, Agents, 38 Chestnut Street, St. Louis; thereby leaving me free to attend exclusively to my missionary duties.

Not only do these letters illustrate the difficulty of locating and securing title to public lands, they are the only mention in Hogan's writings of names of prospective colonists. A search of the Bureau of Land Management's transactions reveals that all but three of these ten Irish pioneers did subsequently succeed in getting titles to other parcels of government land. Their new tracts were not in the area Hogan had favored for the locus of his settlement. Most were in the rougher terrain of Oregon or Ripley County or to a lesser extent, Carter or Shannon County.

32
Centrevi
Ala Mode
31
Anna
Eminence
30
Barnesvi
SHANNON
Current
29
Copper
Piedm
nTown
Chiltons
Regionville
Glen Dale
28
Henpeck
Greenwoo
Valle
Van Buren
27
Mill
Birch Tree
Davis
Pipe Creek
26
CARTE
Lowassie
25
Thomasville
Woodside
Father
Hogans
Settlement
24
Mill
Alton
Eleven Point
RIP
Engleside
23
Webster
Gatewood
22
Mill
Creek

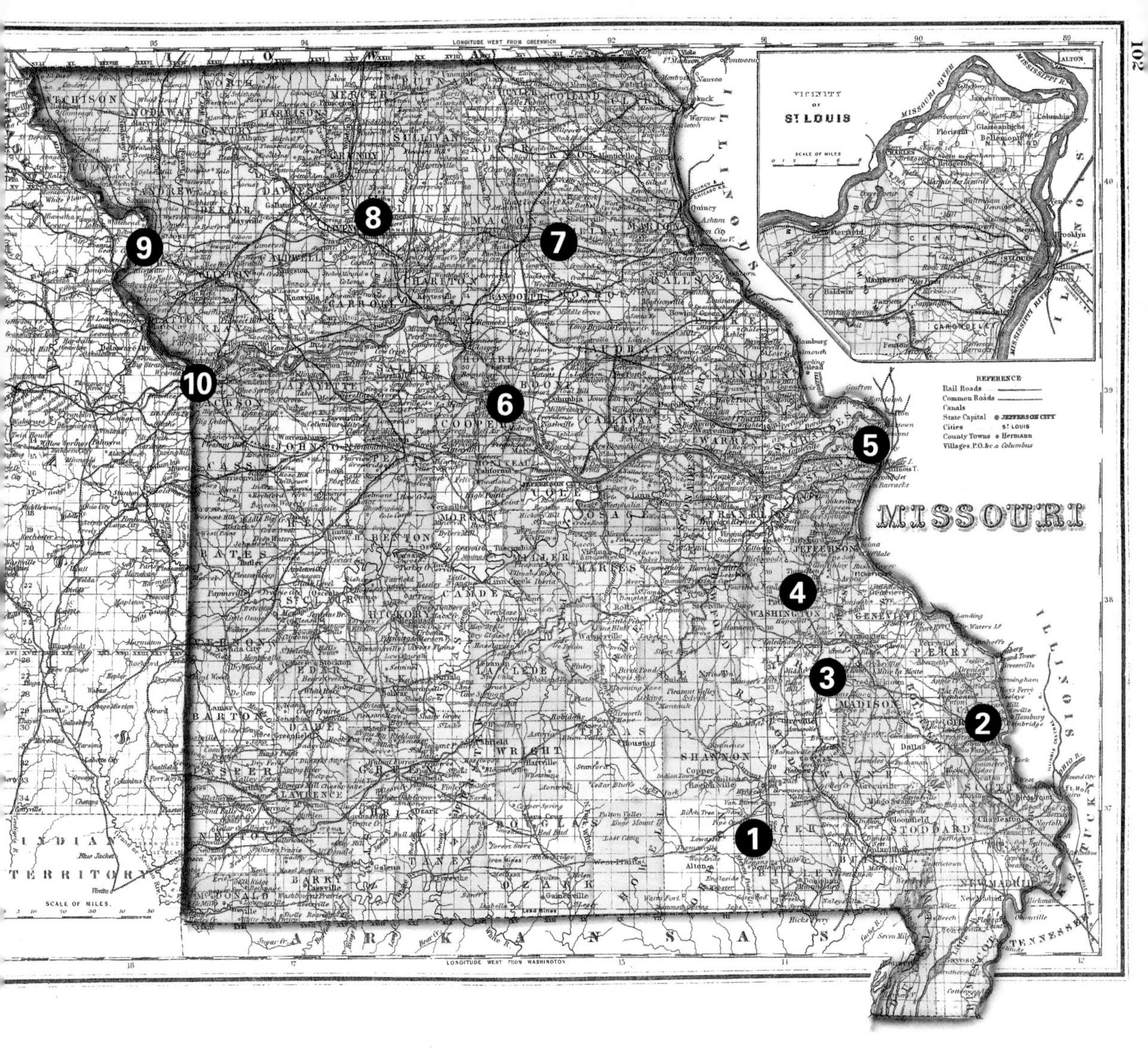

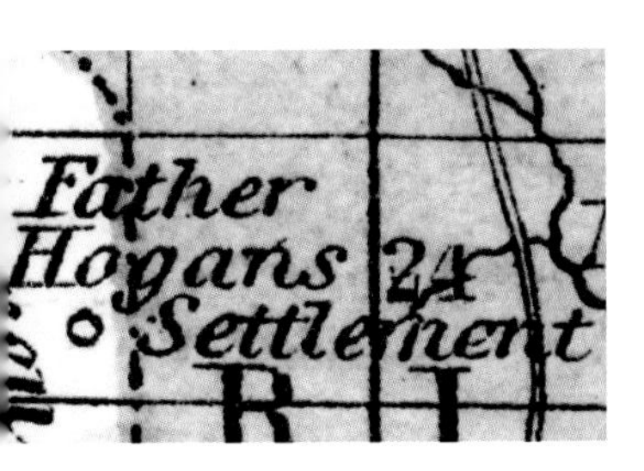

Maps located Father Hogan's Settlement years after its demise. This Colton's Missouri Map of 1875 correctly locates the church property on the Oregon/Ripley county line about twenty miles north of Arkansas. The 1866 Colton's Sectional Map (detail below) called the colony "Father Hogan's Irish Settlement". Courtesy Miller Nichols Library Special Collections, University of Missouri Kansas City.

1. **Hogan's Settlement**
2. **Jackson Land Office**
3. **Ironton**
4. **Old Mines**
5. **St. Louis**
6. **Missouri River**
7. **Hannibal-St. Joseph RR**
8. **Chillicothe**
9. **St. Joseph**
10. **Kansas City**

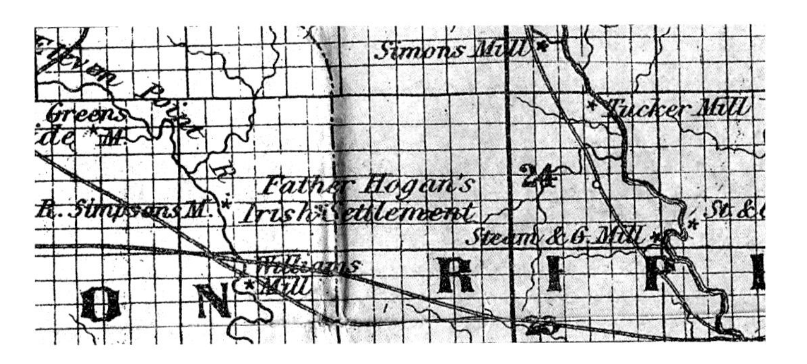

Upon return from his effort to buy government land in the Ozarks, Father Hogan's mission in northwest Missouri began to show signs of life. On the empty lot in Chillicothe a church was built, but not without problems. A man from Chicago "who made preferential claims for the job because he was a Catholic" built an unusable foundation:

> Afterwards, skipping from town, he (the dishonest contractor) sought pastures new, hoping no doubt, in a world full of fools, soon to find another verdant young clergyman. Arriving home, I went to inspect the work, and found that I could kick it to pieces with the heel of my boot. I soon, however, had the rotten stone and crumbling wall rebuilt with better material, and by an honest mechanic.

The "verdant young clergyman" also criticized a local nativist secret society from the pulpit. The lodge members retaliated by breaking the new church's stained glass windows:

> Alas, the windows which were really beautiful were not suffered to shower their rainbow tints very long over the secluded little sanctuary. A rather too warm sermon from the fervid young missionary, against forbidden secret societies, brought the gentlemen of grips and signs to visit his chapel at the midnight hour, and to belabor with barbarous sticks and guns, the artistic little gems, brought like pearls from afar, that were willing to live on and shine for God, even in the depths of the wilderness. Chillicothe's first little Catholic church had to humble itself to the level of its surroundings. Henceforward its windows were to be of vulgar glass. By great efforts, and by collections made near and far, the little church was completed. The church lot, too, was fenced, and all was paid for, so far as I knew. It was a strong tie for the hearts of Catholic people,

The Eleven Point River runs only four miles west of the site of Father Hogan's church and is the western boundary of the official Irish Wilderness. Most of the rest of the river in Missouri is within the National Scenic Riverway system managed by the U.S. Forest Service.

Although the rivers that flow through the Irish Wilderness are fed by some of America's largest springs, Hogan curiously mentions only the ready availability of water from small springs. Greer Springs pumps an average of 214 million gallons a day of cold, clear water into the Eleven Point River.

> to stop there and settle, as many of them did from that day forward.

At this point, John Joseph Hogan felt free to attend to his colony of Irish immigrants in the Ozark wilderness. His dilemma of having founded frontier missions at opposite corners of a big undeveloped state was becoming apparent:

> The completion of the little church at Chillicothe gave me opportunity to pay some attention to the many calls on me from another direction. These calls came from the settlers lately moved into southern Missouri, who claimed that I should attend them or get another priest to do so. I presented the case to His Grace the Most Reverend Archbishop of St. Louis, with request that he send a priest to take charge of the

A few tracts were acquired east of the Current River, but most of the Irish settlement lay west. The National Park Service's Ozark National Scenic Riverway extends into the region of Irish land purchases. Most canoers prefer the faster river upstream. The area Hogan's group settled is near the southern boundary of the Ozark uplift and the rivers slow down as the relief diminishes.

mission begun at Chillicothe, so as to leave me free to attend the new mission in southern Missouri. His Grace replied that he had not priests enough to attend the missions, that all the priests of the diocese were engaged on duties from which not one could be spared, and that, besides, he did not know that he could find a priest willing to engage in such purposes as I was in pursuit of. Not disconcerted, I resolved not to abandon either place. Without apology or explanation forgoing from Chillicothe, and without being able to conjecture my future movements which I placed in submission to the will of God, I set out towards the South in the end of the month of November, 1858. Traveling through the counties of Livingston, Linn, Chariton and Randolph, I got on the cars at Sturgeon in Boone County, which was then the terminus of the North Missouri Railway. Arrived in St. Louis, I took, the Iron Mountain Railway cars to Pilot Knob, and from there I traveled by wagon into southern Missouri.

Previously Hogan had reported that his colonists' applications for land on the tributaries of the Black River in Carter County had been denied. Now he was disappointed to find that all of the government property there had been taken. Hogan was certainly an idealist, but he also had

Hills along the Eleven Point River, looking south toward Arkansas, on the Ripley/Oregon county line. Three miles north, Father Hogan built his log church.

a farmer's practicality. He knew land. Earlier Hogan had remarked that buying private property, already improved, seemed a bargain in southern Missouri. Others—Archbishop Kenrick? the settlers?—were attracted to the cheaper government wilderness land. He moved the colony, "very much against my will," further into the wilds. Under the heading, "A Difficulty," he describes the dilemma:

> Arrived at the settlement, I found a difficulty existing. In the district of country where I had bought land the year previous, intending to make the place the center of the proposed settlement, I found that all the government land, fit for cultivation, had in the meantime been bought by parties not Catholics, so that there was no longer a possibility of owning sufficient ground there to form a colony such as I had contemplated. There was improved land enough in the neighborhood that could be bought at a reasonable price and on easy conditions. But the cry was for government land and at government price. Westward then, though very much

Large springs have already contributed to the base flow of the Current River when Big Springs adds an average of 286 million gallons of water a day. After heavy rains in the surrounding hills, this can grow to nearly a billion gallons. Measurements are difficult as the river floods the spring in high water as seen here. Big Spring is the largest in Missouri, followed by Greer Springs.

against my will, I had to move about forty miles, to a region of country where there was yet much vacant government land, on the confines of Ripley and Oregon counties, along the tributaries of the Current and Eleven Point rivers, about twenty miles north of the state of Arkansas.

THE NEW SETTLEMENT

Even today the country between the Current and Eleven Point rivers is heavily forested and sparsely populated. Hardwoods mixed with pines have replaced the pure stands of giant shortleaf pine that Hogan noted. It is mostly hilly, but there are some undissected uplands that Hogan and the surveyor had located on his journeys. When the entries he wanted most had been sold, Hogan directed his land agent to buy these relatively level tracks between the rivers:

> On a wide and fair tract of ground bought and donated by Reverend James Fox of Old Mines, Missouri, a one story log house forty feet square was erected and partitioned into two apartments, one for a chapel and the other for the priest's residence. Soon improvements went on apace; cutting down trees, splitting rails, burning brushwood, making fences, grubbing roots and stumps, building houses, digging wells, opening roads, breaking and ploughing land, and sowing crops. Already in the spring of 1859, there were about forty families on the newly acquired government lands, or on improved farms purchased, east and west of Current River, in the counties of Ripley and Oregon; and many more were coming, so that the settlement was fairly striding towards final success.
>
> The little chapel amid the forest trees in the wilderness was well attended. Mass, sermon, catechism, confessions, devotions, went on as in old congregations. The quiet solitariness of the place seemed to inspire devotion. Nowhere could the human soul so profoundly worship as in the depths of that leafy forest, beneath the swaying branches of the lofty oaks and pines, where solitude and the heart of man united in praise and wonder of the Great Creator.

Father James Fox was issued a land patent on September 1, 1859 for 320 acres in Oregon County. The Irish pastor of Old Mines and Potosi donated it for the colony's use. On this site, a forty-foot square log chapel and priest's quarters were built by Father Hogan. On May 17, 1879, the property was sold for back taxes. For a long time, the outline of the church's stone foundation was a visitable feature in "the priest's field." Through the years, the rocks have been appropriated for other building uses or removed to facilitate plowing. It is today a fescue pasture.

Paid for Church

700 feet plank	$[illegible]7-00
2000 boards at 62 per hun	12-40
1000 Do. lost by fire	6-20
hauling lumber 4 day at 2	8-00
hauling Shingles 1 day	2-00
D° logs for floor 1 "	2-00
D° logs for building 3	6-00
4 days notching 126½	5-6
½ day hewing	-65
man roofing 4 days	4-00
400 feet plank	4-00
hauling Same	2-80
Building fire place	3-50
Nails + hardware	5-00
Calicoes Candlestick &c for altar	5-50
Altar linens	2-00
	$85-31

Rec^d for the Church

D. Fleming	$1-00
D. Quinlan	1-00
Rev. J. Fox	17-00
Rev Mr. Walsh	
paid in all #20	
ded - [illegible] - 10-55	
Serv - 3-00	
affid - 50	
1 trip 4 days 3-00	
2 D° 1-50	
$18-55 bal	1-45
Re J. O'Sullivan	20-00
Rev D J. Lillis	20-00
Madame Lamorque	10
Miss Detchemendy	5
	$75-45

What does a log church in the wilderness cost? And how does a pioneer priest pay for it? In the archives of the St. Louis Archdiocese is a small notebook, likely carried by Hogan in a saddlebag during the years the colony was in the wilderness. Many clergymen might envy his church building deficit of only $9.86. Throughout his career, Hogan remained fiscally conservative. Courtesy of the Archdiocese of St. Louis Archives.

Father Hogan's sketch of "society in southern Missouri" is singularly uncritical of pioneer Ozark culture which even then was rapidly becoming anachronistic. Most written accounts of these plain folks are patronizing if not contemptuous. Of largely Scotch Irish stock these westering southern highlanders were independent to a fault, unashamedly poor, and indifferent to the opinions of their betters. Early travel writers often stressed the crudeness of locals in order to exaggerate the traveler's travails. This is not to say the folks of the hills and hollows could not on occasion be intransigent. Hogan clearly admired them, but he was atypical of the educated profiler of frontier life. From his writings, it is clear he was plainspoken, unpretentious, and had a self-deprecating sense of humor. The adventurous young Irish-born priest and the Ozark pioneers shared common democratic values:

> In keeping with these scenes were the simple, quiet ways of the early settlers of southern Missouri, who were mostly

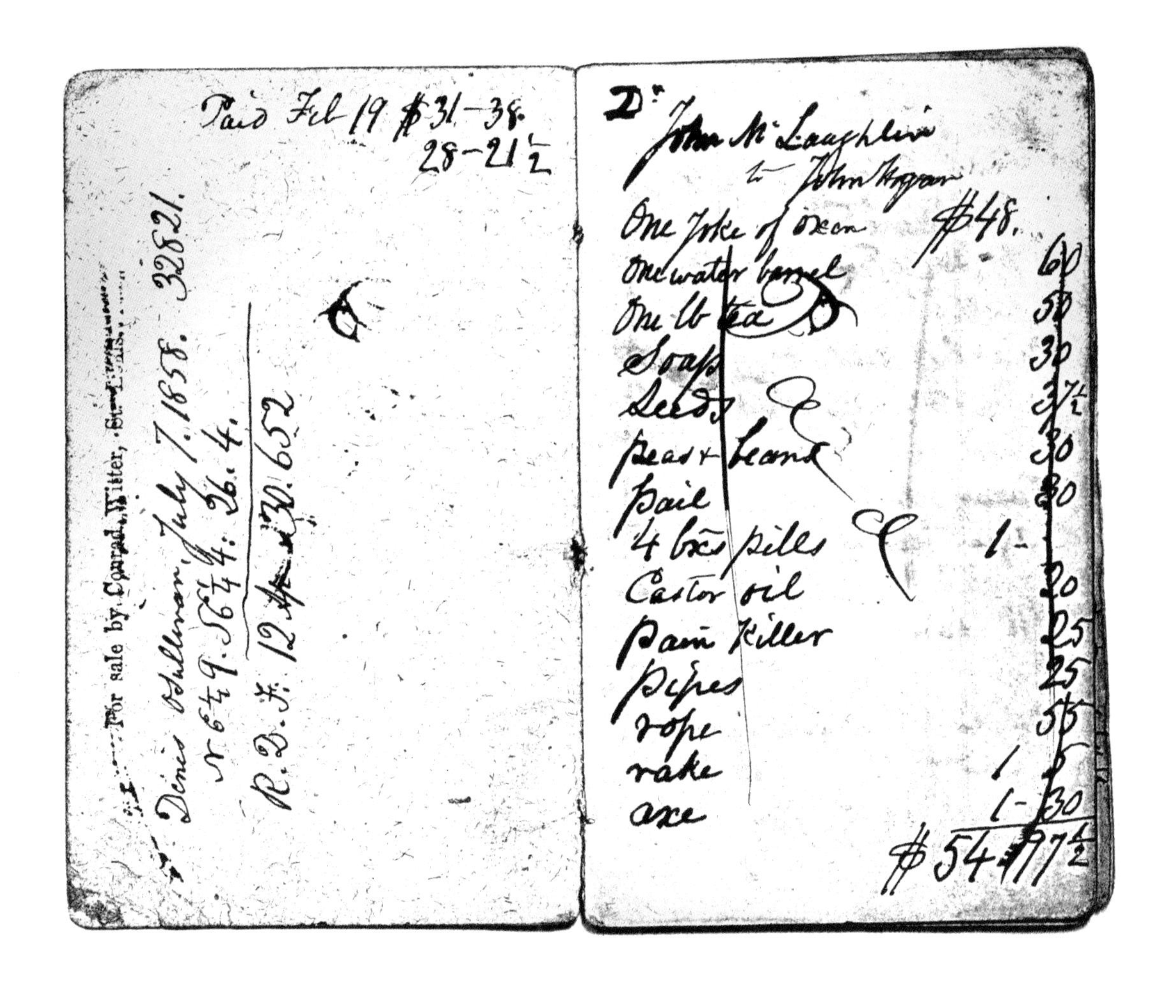

Paid Feb 19 $31-38
28-21½

For sale by Conrad Witter, St. Louis.

Dr John McLaughlin
to John Hogan

One Yoke of oxen	$48.
One water barrel	60
One lb tea	50
Soap	30
Seeds	37½
Peas & beans	30
Pail	30
4 boxes pills	1-
Castor oil	20
Pain Killer	25
Pipes	25
rope	55
rake	1-
axe	1-30
	$54-77½

Other pages of the little notebook detail a pioneer priest's necessities, including a yoke of oxen ($48), one water barrel (60 cents), soap, seeds, castor oil, pain killer and a $1.30 axe. Courtesy of the Archdiocese of St. Louis Archives.

from North Carolina and Tennessee, and of whom much may be said in praise. They were kindhearted, honest, sincere and sociable. No stranger ever traveled amongst them without feeling his heart warmed with the fullest conviction, that, if worthy his presence gave them pleasure, that he was treated to the best they had or could afford, and that his person, money and property were safe and sacred in their keeping. Vice was little known amongst them. Intemperance was nowhere observable, although they usually took as a matter of course, their morning dram, or a drop with a friend, from a keg of the best, distilled by themselves or by some neighbor willing to share or barter on accommodating terms. Every one smoked, men and women, young and old. The weed grew abundantly, and was usually the best tended patch of crop on the place. There was no need of manufactured tobacco or of fancy pipes. Home growth and home manufacture found favor. Corncob pipes were easily made, and for pipe stems cane was abundant. It grew along the streams and by the water's side. The maidens, and swains married young, usually before

> twenty, often at sixteen, and their married life was remarkably virtuous and happy. The marriage dowry was usually a one room log house. The young man was fortuned by his father with a yoke of oxen and a plow. The bride was dowered by her mother with wealth of homespun dresses and household fabrics of like manufacture. Timber from a neighboring saw-mill was easily framed into a variety of articles of household furniture, and the eyes of the young couple were none the less delighted with it, for being pure of veneer or varnish, of which their rural surroundings gave them no knowledge whatever. Uncle Sam had given them a homestead of three hundred and twenty acres, at twelve and a half cents per acre. There was no reason in the world why they should not be happy. Moreover, the young wife had been taught by her mother to knit, spin, weave and sew. The young husband had been taught by his father to tend sheep and cattle, and to cultivate cotton and corn. The education of husband and wife could be depended upon to procure them a living. The plow cultivated plots and furrows in the field. The wheel and loom wrought fabrics at home. There was no need of the merchant's ship, bringing goods from afar. No need of town fashions, or of store clothes. Willing hands and humble hearts made the one-room log cabin a sacred place and a happy home.

Hogan noted the early settlers of the region were "mostly from North Carolina and Tennessee." Kentucky, Virginia and Alabama also contributed westward migrating homesteaders to the mix. Others came from Illinois and Indiana but they originated in the southern highlands too. Most were descendants of Protestant Scots who had been invited by King James the First to settle confiscated rebel Catholic properties in Northern Ireland in the 1600s. A quarter of a million Scotch-Irish came to the new world a century later, when the English raised rents and imposed tariffs.

With a long history of living along conflicted borders, a distrust of central authority, and strong individualistic personalities, the Scotch-Irish evolved into prototypical American pioneers. Generations of frontier living in the Appalachians probably blurred their awareness of the specifics of their European past. Originally Presbyterian, most were now Baptist or Methodist. Hogan's account that many of the Irish colony's neighbors claimed they had Irish Catholic ancestry challenges standard history:

> The old settlers were anxious to get acquainted with the priest, many of them having traveled quite a distance for the purpose. Their manner showed curiosity more than prejudice towards the Catholic Church. Many of them said, as their names indicated, and as was told them by their parents, that they were descendants of Irish Catholics, who had been driven or forced to emigrate in early times. They could not explain why they were not Catholics, as their forefathers were, except by the fact that there were no priests or Catholic churches where they and their parents for generations were brought up. They had therefore fallen in with the prevailing churches of their surroundings. In the course of a short time, as acquaintance progressed, I was invited by some families to visit them. From these visits resulted wishes and requests to be instructed in the Catholic religion and received into the Church. This aroused the displeasure and opposition of the preachers, of whom there were several in the neighborhood.

In north Missouri, John Hogan criticized the Know-Nothings, a nativist, anti-immigrant movement, and they retaliated by breaking the new church's stained glass windows. When he began instructions on conversion to Catholicism in his southern colony, local preachers became threatened. Pioneer Ozark religious institutions were subject to schisms and fractures. Ministers often lured members from other congregations by exaggerating minor denominational differences. Roman Catholicism presented a larger target for invidious comparison. For proselytizing ministers, Hogan may have appeared to be a godsend:

> The preachers began to hold meetings and revivals near the Catholic settlement, and in those places where the parties lived who were known to be inclining towards the Catholic Church. At one of these meetings, a preacher named Tim Reeves, who was afterwards a notorious guerilla leader during the war, delivered the following discourse, aimed directly at some persons before him, who were then preparing for baptism in the Catholic Church, and who reported his words to me. "Wait," said he, "until the Catholic Church gets hold on some of you, and then you will know what it is to be a Catholic. I was at Cape Girardeau a short time ago. There is a big Catholic church at Cape Girardeau, and the place is full of Romanists. I went to the church and stood near the door to see what was going on. The old priest had an image, which he held up in his hands, for the people to adore. The old priest had

> it so fixed on wires, that whatever he said, the imago would say it after him. Then the people threw themselves down on their faces, and gave the old priest lots of money. Do you want to belong to that old priest, and to the idolatrous Church of Rome, that makes the people adore images in order to cheat them out of their money?"

One of John Joseph Hogan's missionary tactics in north Missouri was to ride into town and after visiting isolated Catholic families give public lectures on his faith. Given his democratic values and sense of humor, he would have been an effective frontier speaker. Probably he relished open exchanges of a theological nature. Hogan does express astonishment at Rev. Tim Reeves' fanciful distortion of Catholicism. The well-educated Irishman obviously wasn't familiar with the legendary ability of hillfolks to spin tall tales:

> The persons who reported this sermon of Tim Reeves to me, were shocked by the accusations he made against the Catholic Church, which they protested they could not believe from him, and that he must have willfully prevaricated. I apologized for Tim Reeves that possibly he may have been in good faith, not knowing the ceremonies of the Catholic Church or their meaning. I explained, that on Good Friday, the day on which our Blessed Lord died for us on the Cross, the Catholic Church commemorated that sacred event by causing to be exposed and held up before the people, a large cross, with the image of Christ crucified upon it. The priest who held up the cross in his arms, said, to the people present, in Latin: "Behold the wood of the Cross, upon which hung the Savior of the world; let us come and adore." Then the deacon, standing near the priest, repeated the same words, in the name of the congregation present. "Behold the wood of the Cross, upon which hung the Savior of the world; come let us adore." It was this answering of the deacon to the priest that made poor ignorant Tim Reeves believe that it was the image that spoke. That is all that poor ignorant Tim Reeves, preacher as he is, knows about the subject. ... What seemed strange, ridiculous, and wicked, to Tim Reeves, was no doubt very pious and praiseworthy, to Catholics. But it would be useless to explain this to such men as he, who can see nothing but malice and wickedness in Catholics and in the Catholic Church.

Civilizing institutions like churches and schools were scarce but valued on the frontier. Catholics' ability to provide both

Hogan's church and the Irish settlers' cabins were doubtlessly constructed of square-hewn oak logs like this 1858 house built by Tennessee settler Luther Parrott. A rare example of a pioneer building it stands in the Big Hurricane Creek valley between Falling Springs Mill and the Eleven Point River.

pieces of social infrastructure prompted resentment from a circuit-riding preacher who claimed to have been offered a teaching job at the colony:

> There was another preacher there, a circuit rider, who, it was said, set himself up to great advantage as an opponent of the Catholic Church. "Priest Hogan," said he, "sent for me, and offered me a large salary to teach school in his settlement. I was about to accept the offer, but when he proposed that I should teach the Romanist catechism, I said no, that I would not teach that wicked catechism were I to get the whole world." Priest Hogan avers that he never saw or spoke to such person that he knows of or can remember.

Father Hogan ends the narration of his longest stay at the Irish settlement with an account of being accosted by a "gigantic, active young man." Hogan confesses he set out on a sick call to a family living on Mill Creek—now called the Middle Fork of the Fourche River—carrying a sword cane:

> Afterwards, as I proceeded, when at about a quarter of a mile distance from my house, I felt very much dissatisfied with myself, and was even shocked to think that I should have with

> me, for my protection, so murderous a weapon, when I should rather depend, and entirely so, on the Real Divine Presence with me when on an errand of mercy. I knew not how or why I felt so fully persuaded. I returned to the house, dismounted from the saddle, put the sword cane back in its place, and resumed my journey.

Returning from the sick call, Hogan stopped to visit a friend, Judge Hutcheson. He asked directions from workmen harvesting wheat. One of them asked to speak privately with the priest. They moved away, out of sight of the others. Sensing danger, Hogan asked his business. The young giant grabbed the horse's bridle. Hogan dismounted and the man "eyed me fiercely with the look of a murderer; and that instant, seizing me in his powerful hands insulted me past all endurance by acts that were disgustingly vile and shockingly brutal. It was the moment to use the sword cane, but I thank God that I had not it." Hogan was "saved from direst harm" by the sudden arrival of Judge Hutcheson. The judge encouraged Hogan to prosecute his assailant, noting there was reason to believe he had been engaged by an ex-preacher and he was a noted criminal who had already served time in the Arkansas penitentiary. Hogan declined to prosecute and forgave the offender.

Apart from friction with circuit-riding preachers, Father Hogan had reason to be optimistic about his colony in the wilderness. Scores of poor Irish families had taken claim on thousands of acres of government land. Hogan and his surveyors had located some tracts with agricultural potential amid millions of acres of virgin forest. If isolated and less fertile than the prairies of north Missouri, it was affordable. Hogan and his land agent would handle the government paper work, but financing would have been necessary. Archbishop Kenrick provided most of the funds. Hogan and other priests added what money they could. Repayment to the Church would be made when possible.

The ambitious southern settlement began to show promise during the months that Hogan worked there. Meanwhile, his mission in northern Missouri began to thrive in an expanding economy. In 1859, the railroad was completed all the way across north Missouri. The 1886 *History of Caldwell and Livingston Counties* describes the excitement:

> The building of the Hannibal and St. Joseph Railroad was of the greatest advantage to the town. Money was plenty and prices good during the construction of the road through the county, and those were flush times. The population increased from 800 to 1,200. From 1,200 in January, 1859, the population increased to 1,800 or 2,000 by January, 1861. Schools and churches were established, business enterprises were inaugurated, and a full tide of prosperity set in and was fast bearing the town on to permanent fortune.

As John Hogan was helping the immigrants build log cabins from the timber they felled to create small fields, his northern Missouri "old friends" were crying for help:

> While these things were going on in the settlement in southern Missouri, I received many letters from those I had left behind me in northern Missouri, complaining that they had not heard Mass or received the Sacraments since I left them, that many had died without the last Sacraments, and that then presently there were many children unbaptized and many sick needing to be prepared for death. I told them to call on Reverend Father Scanlon of St. Joseph, and Reverend Father Murphy of Hannibal to attend them, especially in sickness. They replied that they had done so, but that these priests could not undertake to leave their own congregations and go on long journeys to others not of their charge, and who should have a priest themselves. I then again laid the wants and complaints of these Catholics of the interior of northwest Missouri before His Grace the Archbishop of St. Louis, who replied as before, that he had no priest to spare to send them, and that he did not know of any priest willing to resign his place. Some time afterwards, however, he informed me that two of the Lazarist Fathers of Cape Girardeau, had promised him, at his request, to go for that one time on a missionary visit to those in whose behalf I had written to him. Accordingly, Rev. T. D. O'Keeffe and Rev. P. McMennamy did set out from Cape Girardeau or the Barrens, and did make a missionary tour through those places where as I had stated, Catholics lived, without having a priest to attend them. Soon again however, the same complaints began to be made as before, and in addition thereto, there was another matter requiring attention.

The "new difficulty" he mentions was that the sawmill owners who had supplied the lumber for the new church in Chillicothe had sent an unanticipated bill for $75. Not

While the rugged terrain of the Ozark Highlands inhibited transportation and challenged settlement, the realist Hogan believed his modest colony of Irish immigrants would ultimately succeed. It would be national political turbulence, not adverse geography or a lack of will, which doomed their brave experiment.

only were the priests in Hannibal and St. Joseph, to whom he wrote for help, preoccupied, they "saw no purpose to make such collections and payment, since, as everyone saw, the church at Chillicothe was given up and abandoned." Threatened with a personal lawsuit over the bill, he rode north on the last days of October, 1859.

> Arrived at Chillicothe, I was received with joy. And it did not take me long to collect the money to pay the saw-mill debt. During the month of November I visited the incipient missions, east and west, and all around, wherever I had heard of Catholics having settled. The joy of having Mass again, caused them to entreat me to stay with them. I expressed the great pleasure it would give me to serve them, but I made them no binding promise.
>
> I set out again for southern Missouri where I stayed the greater part of December, attending, among other duties, to the instruction of some converts heretofore partly prepared and now baptized and received into the Church. My recent

Chillicothe, located on a level, fertile prairie, entered an era of rapid growth when the Hannibal and St. Joseph Railroad arrived. Some of the Irish railroad workers that Father Hogan ministered to would stay and become his parishioners. Once Hogan built a church, Catholics of other national origins were attracted as well. The population at the outbreak of the Civil War approached 2,000.

visit to North Missouri impressed me with the idea that the increasing number of Catholics there, could not be neglected, much less totally abandoned. The time too seemed ripe for building more churches in northern Missouri. The children there needed to be instructed for First Communion and Confirmation, and the church at Chillicothe was yet without the sacred rite of dedication.

For these purposes, and for such time, longer or shorter, as it would take me to accomplish them, I was again northward bound. Unlike the happy little birds of spring and autumn, ever hying their way in season to more genial climes, it was my untoward fate, poor bird of passage that I was, to face northward, and out of season, against cold wintry blasts. The last days of December, 1859, found me again in Chillicothe, meditating much work to do.

Never again would John Joseph Hogan see his Irish colonists in the Ozark wilderness.

ONE HUNDRED MILES OF FIRE

With the completion of the Hannibal and St. Joseph Railroad, there was an influx of settlers. Father Hogan returned from his extended stay at his southern colony to find a growing demand for his services. Catholics of German, French, and Canadian as well as American and Irish origin were attracted to the area in part due to the availability of a priest. At the same time, great social and political pressures were about to erupt that would complicate his mission in north Missouri and greatly imperil the wilderness Irish settlement:

> Eighteen hundred and sixty from beginning, to end was a year of tremendous excitement and inauspicious portent. Four great national parties, having their respective political platforms and chosen leaders, entered the arena contending for dominancy. But one party could be victorious. The vanquished, or those who so considered themselves, rushed on to the bad principle of national disruption. The party elected to office aligned itself, as in duty bound, to defend national unity. Peace proposals were flung to the winds. The sword was drawn to decide the issue. Thirty millions of people begirding themselves with deadly weapons and falling into antagonistic battle lines, their hearts filled with hatred of each other, was a scene that can never be witnessed again until the world's final tribulation has come. Property became at once of no value. Home afforded no shelter. Friendship, and even the closest family ties, fell off into party lines. Churches and schools, religious and benevolent associations, public works and private enterprises, were suddenly suspended or paralyzed. All that was, was comprehended in one word—war. The tread and tramp of armies on foot and on horseback, the clatter of cannon wheels and the clacking of weapons, the hoarse commands of military

Flanking the monument to General Sterling Price are hundreds of headstones of unknown rebel volunteers killed at the Battle of Wilson's Creek in 1861. His pro-Confederate Missouri State Guard won, but seven months later at Pea Ridge, Arkansas, Union forces defeated the region's Confederate Army. For the rest of the conflict, federal troops controlled Missouri's rivers and railroads. St. Louis and many population centers were Union garrisons. Most rural Missourians were not for secession but they disdained abolitionists' notions and despised the occupying Union forces. Small but deadly bands of partisans (guerrillas) sniped at the federals, bringing about savage reprisals.

TO THE MEMORY OF THE MISSOURI SOLDIER IN THE ARMY
OF THE
CONFEDERATE STATES OF AMERICA
MAJOR GENERAL STERLING PRICE

MISSIONARY TIME TABLE.

On days not herein stated, and excepting railroad schedule time for traveling to and from places herein mentioned, the Priest may be found at his place of residence, Chillicothe.

APPOINTMENTS FOR —MASS— 1860.	Chillicothe	Macon City	Brookfield	Mexico	Cameron
January	1	8	15	22	29
February	5	12	19	26	
March	4	11	18	25	
April	1	8	15	22	29
May	6	13	20	27	
June	3	10	17	24	
July	1	8	15	22	29
August	5	12	19	26	
September	2	9	16	23	30
October	7	14	21	28	
November	4	11	18	25	
December	2	9	16	23	30
Appointments for Mass on holidays and week days will be otherwise made and communicated.	1st Sunday	2nd Sunday	3rd Sunday	4th Sunday	5th Sunday

This ambitious printed schedule may explain why Father Hogan didn't travel to his Irish colony in 1860. By the summer of 1861, the hostilities of the Civil War would have made the journey impossible. Still, it is puzzling that his book contains virtually no mention of the settlement after his return to Chillicothe in December, 1859.

men marshaling their forces, made a constant din and a never-ending pageant. Soon, with appalling force, the two tidal waves of wrath and power fell upon each other. Out from their recoil came the shouts of victory and the moans of defeat; and, with both, the wails and cries of widows and orphans, to whom the strife, end as it may, could bring no hope or comfort. The peacefully inclined fled in terror whithersoever they could, to places of safety—to the Pacific shores, to the Canada borders, to countries beyond the sea.

The railroad that had created opportunities on the prairies of north Missouri now became a strategic asset and a military target:

> The call of the President of the United States for men to maintain the Union and to recover its forts and arsenals, though refused by the Missouri Rebel Governor, was responded to nevertheless by the people of Missouri, who were loyal to the Union, and who formed themselves into military organizations in aid of the United States. To the aid of these came the regiments from Illinois, Iowa and Kansas, quickly mustered into service in answer to the President's call; their first duty being to maintain and keep open the railways lately built through Northern Missouri, and now used to convey Union troops to the front to resist the rebellion onset. On the other hand, the great body of Missourians who had resolved to stand by the South, in obedience to calls for troops from their leaders, Governor Jackson and General Price, had likewise formed themselves into battalions and regiments, their first assigned duty being to destroy the lines of communication that the Union men had aligned themselves to defend. Hence the first fierce war struggles in North Missouri occurred in my mission, along the lines of the Hannibal & St. Joseph and the North Missouri Railways; the passing trains being fired upon from every convenient ambush, and the bridges and trestles being burnt and rebuilt many times in succession. No one then traveling on these railways could be sure of his life for one minute. And many a life was lost by the flying bullets that smashed and splintered through the cars, and by the derailed trains hurled down over precipices and embankments.
>
> Owing to the incapacity, and perplexity of plans and purposes, of the many Federal Generals set up and suspended in Missouri in 1861, the state was in the greatest confusion and uncertainty as to its future. The confusion was at its height,

> and was general throughout the state, after the Federal defeats at Wilson's Creek and Lexington. There seemed then no hope whatever of peace. And no one could forecast results.

Father Hogan relocated to Macon City "to be more centrally located in my mission." There he observed multitudes of north Missourians who "had followed Price at Boonville, Wilson's Creek and Lexington, flooding home, tired (as they said) of the war, and resolved henceforth to live and die in peace with all men." They were, in fact, Confederate saboteurs:

> All of a sudden their real purpose flashed out to heaven, in the light of all that was combustible of one hundred miles of the North Missouri Railroad, stretching out from Macon City towards St. Louis—ablaze at the same moment and as if ignited by one hand. Telegraph poles were cut down as if by the single stroke of an ax; and the wire, broken and in coils, was hauled away several miles, into the woods and fields. Bridges, culverts, trestles, tanks, station houses, were all set on fire. Yokes of oxen were harnessed to the ties, which were hauled out of place, then piled together to burn; and on the blazing heaps, the railroad iron, molten red in the center, fell down at the ends in crooks and twists, thereby rendering it unfit for use, until taken to some rolling mill or foundry to be straightened or recast. Not less than ten thousand men, acting in concert along that hundred miles, could have in the space of two or three hours produced so dire results. The plan was deep laid, the secret well kept, and the work thoroughly done. The confederate spies were soon back to their camp again, without loss of a man. The end of 1861 found me residing still at Macon City, to which place, as already stated, I had moved from Chillicothe after the fall of Lexington. My change of place of residence, in so far as I had hoped to be in greater safety, was a disappointment. The one hundred miles of burning railroad, between me and St. Louis, showed clearly that the smoke of battle had changed from front to rear. So "about face" I marched back again to Chillicothe.

Although the railroad was frequently attacked by rebels, it was repaired and kept more or less operational. A federal garrison in Chillicothe protected the railroad and provided some stability. At least the town wasn't burned to the ground by federal troops as were all of the courthouse villages associated with Hogan's Irish colony in the Ozarks.

Chillicothe Catholic elementary school named for Bishop John Joseph Hogan. In Kansas City, Hogan Preparatory Academy, originally named Bishop Hogan High School, is now a charter school run by the University of Central Missouri. Courtesy Kansas City-St. Joseph Diocese Archives.

Nevertheless, times were hard, people distraught. Local institutions were disrupted. Father Hogan responded by providing a school for the children of the entire community:

> The financial straits, together with the civil and social disturbances caused by the war, brought the educational interests of the country into a very disorganized condition. In the rural districts and country towns the schools without funds or teachers, were generally suspended. In consequence, the children, instead of acquiring the learning and disciplined habits necessary for them, went about idle and uninstructed, associating with dangerous companions, and engaging in the exciting war talk everywhere prevalent at the time. The girls swayed by the party bias of their parents and relatives, contended with their companions, and often in angry words, as their preferences or family ties allied them to one or the other of the warring sections. The boys, breaking away from all restraint, formed opposing camps, and under their chosen leaders, assaulted each other with as varying results of victory or defeat, as the armies at Richmond and Shiloh. In this state of things the parents, Catholic and non-Catholic alike, besought me to take the children under my care, and to rescue them from the disorderly habits in which they were growing up.

In a neglected public building Hogan taught "Catechism,

Bible History, Greek, Latin, French, Rhetoric, Geometry, Algebra, Grammar, Elocution, Philosophy, Reading, Writing, Arithmetic, Lessons in Music" for two years until the public school system was reorganized. He reported proudly that the education "went on unceasingly, as whirring machinery in a great factory or cotton mill." Father Hogan had pleasant memories of the school having "got the hopeful twigs where I could bend them to some purpose."

Throughout the war John Joseph Hogan extensively crisscrossed his large north Missouri mission territory. Attending the needs of his far-flung parishes, Hogan rode the rails, surviving "twenty-one railroad wrecks of more or less destructiveness." If the Union held the rivers and towns, Confederate guerrillas continued to attack troops and trains. "But the cruelest of their deeds was the massacre at Centralia in September, 1864, of which I barely escaped being a victim." The train that followed the one Hogan rode was attacked by guerrillas on September 27, 1864. Known as the Centralia Massacre, Bloody Bill Anderson's Confederate partisans murdered twenty-two unarmed federal troops riding on the train. As he wrote:

> "Had I waited or been delayed at Martinsburg or Mexico for that train, and had the federal military passes that I carried, been found me, which certainly have happened, as the pockets and pocket-books of all passengers were searched, there is no doubt whatever that I would have shared the fate of the poor fellows who fell on that occasion."

Union Major A.V.E. Johnston pursued Anderson's bushwhackers with a unit of the 39th Missouri Mounted Infantry. Mostly they were farm boys from the region armed with single shot rifles. Jesse James, one of Anderson's guerrillas, is said to have dropped Major Johnston with a pistol shot to the forehead. Of the 155 Union troops Anderson's men ambushed 123 were killed and scalped or beheaded. In 1873, seventy-nine of the bodies that had been hastily buried were dug up for re-interment in the national cemetery at Jefferson City. Grave diggers reported the skeletons were small, indicating youth. All the skulls had a bullet hole.

WAR'S DEVASTATIONS

Late in the war, General Sterling Price's army attacked the Union fort at Ironton. After a costly but unsuccessful Confederate assault, the Union troops fled at night, blowing up the powder magazine as they left. The hole caused by the earth-shattering explosion is still visible at Ft. Davidson State Park. During the skirmish in the surrounding hills, Major Wilson, leader of the raiders of the lower Current and Eleven Point river country, was captured by the Rebs and turned over to Col. Tim Reeves. Wilson and six of his men were later shot by Reeves. The Union Army retaliated with a public execution in St. Louis of six Confederate prisoners.

Relocating Irish immigrants from railroad gangs and city jobs into wilderness homesteads had been an ambitious undertaking. There were many dedicated Irish Catholic priests concerned with the plight of their recently arrived poor fellow countrymen. Few, however, possessed John Hogan's talents as an explorer, horseman, and appraiser of agrarian possibilities in raw land. The colony in the rugged hills between the Eleven Point and Current rivers was up and running when Hogan rode north in December 1859. By the end of the Civil War, his settlement had vanished. It was a painful loss:

> Alas! The devastations of war and the woes and sorrows that follow after it. Who now will build up those waste places? Who now will lead back the poor scattered settlers to their humble but ruined homes? Who now will rekindle for them the light of faith or preach the word of God to them in their little chapel beneath the pines in the forest? Has all that was done and endured there, been for nothing? Is there no hope for a place once so dear and so sacred? To the most adorable will of God, whose ways are ever full of mercy and above our understanding, we most profoundly bow.

John Hogan admitted he had no first-hand knowledge of the Irish settlement during the war years:

> Missouri as a Border State, and consequently as a battle-ground, lost its tens of thousands—fully as many by flight as by combat. My poor settlements suffered irretrievably. The one in Southern Missouri especially became broken and scattered; all who could, having fled therefrom. Ripley County, in which my Southern Settlement was principally located, suffered

> more than any other part of the State. Campbell's Gazetteer of Missouri, in a few words, records its sad fate. "The County suffered severely during the Civil War, being occupied alternately by both armies, besides being invaded by marauding parties and bushwhackers, who murdered peaceful citizens, and destroyed houses, fences, and crops, until towards the close of the war scarcely a male citizen was permitted to remain at home, unmolested. The County Seat was first pillaged and then burned, only two or three houses of the entire town being saved." From cavalry soldiers on duty in that county I learned that corn to feed their horses had to be carried by them in sacks behind them on their horse's backs a distance of eighty miles; not so much as an ear of corn being left, that they could find, in that whole country.

In recent years, local historians have reconstructed a more detailed history of the region where Father Hogan's settlement was located. Union troops, for instance, may have murdered some of his settlers. It was the federals that likely burned their cabins and his log church, not "marauding parties and bushwhackers."

Local historian, Lewis A. Simpson, in his book *Oregon County's Three Flags*, relates a story told by old-timer Cal Ross to Uncle Dave Woodring whose family once owned the land Hogan's church was on:

> While threshing wheat with a groundhog thresher near the Hogan settlement late in the fall of 1863 when federal troops scouting the area came on a group of the Irish, opened fire and killed four of the number, and soon after the remainder of the colony disappeared.

Woodring recalled there was once a stone marker with a chiseled cross at the site, but he could no longer remember the location.

Specifics of what happened to the settlement would have appalled the priest who carried a federal military pass. The Catholic Church hierarchy was sensitive to criticism that it would act as a political not religious institution, so clergy were instructed not to express any controversial views on slavery—either pro or con. For that reason, Father Hogan avoided public expression of his views, but he was sympathetic to the mistreatment of blacks and strongly

Both sides "requisitioned" (i.e. pillaged) from farmers. The taking of food and livestock by Union forces shown in this *Harper's* engraving was particularly resented. Many federal soldiers were from out of state or were the unpopular German immigrants. Most rural Missourians, even if not secessionist, viewed such troops as invaders.

against slavery.

At least one of the settlers, Patrick Griffin, enlisted in the regular Confederate Army. Other Irish colonists it seemed joined the 15th Missouri Cavalry Regiment, a local southern-sympathizing militia. This Ripley County unit was commanded by Tim Reeves, the Baptist preacher whose malicious anti-Catholic rhetoric had incensed Father Hogan. A St. Louis Union newspaper lumped Tim Reeves with the infamous William Clarke Quantrill and Bloody Bill Anderson, blasting the "scoundrely and murderous operations of these guerrilla chieftains."

North Missouri could be dangerous, as Father Hogan discovered, but the entire population was not embroiled in the turmoil as was the case in southeast Missouri. The Hannibal and St. Joseph Railroad ran through Chillicothe. At the outbreak of war the town was taken by the 16th Illinois and occupied throughout the conflict. As the 1886 Livingston County history stated, "Chillicothe came out of the conflict remarkably well. None of her citizens were ruthlessly murdered, only one building—the M. E. Church South—was said to have been burned by the federal soldiers, and in this instance the charge was not proven."

The sparsely settled wilderness where Hogan's settlement was located had no such strategic value. The Iron Mountain Railroad had only reached Pilot Knob some seventy hard miles to the northeast and protected by Fort Davidson. If the rugged Ozarks had scant intrinsic military value, it was worrisome to the Union. In the log cabin homesteads and villages of the Ozarks were thousands of men and boys who were perceived to be a threat to the federal cause.

There were a few secessionists among native Ozarkers who enlisted in the cause of the South and fought far from home in regular Confederate units. Most south Missouri folk just wished the war would go away so they could concentrate on wresting a living from their rocky circumstances. Hogan wrote of the "simple, quiet ways of the early settlers of southern Missouri." Threatened by outsiders, however, they reluctantly joined or supported anti-Union home guard militias.

According to the 2003 *History & Families Ripley County, Missouri,* Reeves' 15th Missouri Cavalry was a mixed blessing. "It was a unit that showed little compassion for the populace it was defending, taking crops, horses and livestock when needed and forcing recruits, willing or unwilling, into its ranks."

The immigrant colonists had even less motivation to take sides than the locals. Nevertheless the roster of Company H of the 15th contained Celtic names like Patrick Martin, Samuel Flannery, Patrick Maoajar, Michael Roney, James Sullivan, and other probable members of Hogan's Irish settlement.

Units such as the 15th Missouri Cavalry operated in a grey area of military legitimacy. Union officers considered them guerrillas and dealt with them as outlaws. The gentlemen of the Confederate high command could scarcely mask their disdain for these poor farmers who were uncommitted to the noble Southern cause. Unable to recruit hill folk into useful regular troops, they were reluctantly given honorific ranks, some money and supplies. They could be useful as scouts and foragers when the Confederate Army attempted its sporadic and unsuccessful raids into Missouri from Arkansas. Guerrilla actions and failed invasions might at least divert Union troops from the eastern theater where the war would be decided.

Within their home territory, the 15th Missouri Cavalry could at times humiliate Union forces sent to discourage cooperation with the Confederates. A combination of rough, forested, familiar terrain and a backwoodsman's skill with weapons sometimes gave the locals an edge over a detachment of Union troops.

The federal response was harsh. Official Union war records contain abundant reports of houses burned and livestock confiscated from suspected guerrillas—the men taken prisoner and "shot while trying to escape."

Captain Robert McElroy's account of an expedition that scouted the Eleven Point River country captures the growing enmity between the Ozarkers and the feds:

> There are no regular organized bands in that part of the country; but any man that can creep on his belly into a camp of federals and steal a horse is entitled to the name and rank of Captain. That portion of the state once cleaned of these marauders, jayhawkers, and thieves, and we will have peace throughout South Missouri. I am of the opinion that the women in that region are even more daring and treacherous, and, in fact, worse than the men, as we found in their possession a number of newly made rebel uniforms, &c.

Captain McElroy reported to Major James Wilson, commanding the Third Missouri State Militia Cavalry at Pilot Knob. Major Wilson was a conflicted man. His brother enlisted in the Confederate Army. His father, also a southern sympathizer, disowned him. The Catholic Major was in the process of divorcing his wife with whom he had two children. Major Wilson's raid in the fall of 1863 may have been the final blow to Father Hogan's colony.

Wilson's official report stated that he left the Union garrison at Pilot Knob on September 28, 1863 with 200 men of the Third Missouri State Militia Cavalry:

> Upon arriving at Falling Springs, I detached Captain [J.W.]. McFaden, with thirty men, with orders to go by way of Boyce's Ford and meet us at Alton. With the remainder of the force crossed the river, about eight miles east, at a place known as Simpkins (Simpsons?) Mill, and also arrived at Alton that p.m. Captain McFaden's command encountered a party of guerrillas, under one Lieutenant Duckworth, whom they routed; as well as capturing several horses, saddles, &c. My immediate command captured 4 guerrillas with their horses, arms, and equipments. From Alton, the third of October, I sent out three scouts, respectively to Boyce's Mill, Simpkins' Mill, and Boyce's Ford, with instructions to scour the country for guerrillas. Captain C. W. Rush, commanding one of these detachments, fell in with the command of Duckworth, whom he succeeded in routing again, besides capturing several horses, camp equipment, &c.

Lieutenant Duckworth was an officer of Company H of Reeves's 15th Missouri Cavalry, the unit that had men with Irish names. As Wilson's orders were to destroy all property of Confederate sympathizers, it has been speculated that Hogan's church and the nearby settlers' cabins were destroyed by Captain Rush's detachment on October 3, 1863. Wilson's report also mentions sending Captain G. L. Herring with eighty men to "escort a train of refugees from Oregon County." Local historians believe these were the remaining colonists of Father Hogan's settlement. The refugees were taken to Pilot Knob and probably released.

Even before the hostilities escalated, Ozark farmers were preyed upon by bandits like Samuel Hildebrand. In his candid autobiography, the notorious guerrilla recalled traveling through Ripley County shortly before Major Wilson's raid. "Here we were detained, for one of my men had the misfortune to lose his horse. Having reached a part of the country known as the Irish Wilderness, we concluded to rest a day and hunt." Hildebrand was paid by the Confederacy to spy on and disrupt the feds, yet he freely admits stealing a replacement horse from a noted local rebel. He did return the horse when chided by other guerrillas.

Both militaries 'requisitioned' (i.e. took what they needed) from settlers. Local Confederate militias and guerrillas didn't burn them out (at times executing the men) as did Union troops.

So brutal and corrupt was the conduct of some federal officers in the wilds of southeast Missouri that the Army brought them up on charges. Several were reprimanded, demoted or discharged.

Tim Reeves personally extracted revenge from Major James Wilson. While leading a cavalry unit protecting Fort Davidson from General Sterling Price's last futile Missouri invasion on September 27, 1864, Wilson was captured. He was never to learn that on that day his divorce from his wife Margaret had become final.

Somehow Tim Reeves, whose unit had joined the raid, got Major Wilson and six of his men turned over to him. Six days later Reeves executed them. Their decomposing, partially hog-eaten bodies were not discovered until October 23.

Incensed, Union General William Rosecrans promptly issued Order 277 requiring one Confederate Major and six enlisted men be "executed by musketry." No Major was in custody, but six randomly selected soldiers from Gratiot Street Prison were taken to Lafayette Park in St. Louis on October 29. Before a crowd of 3,000, the unfortunate and completely uninvolved prisoners of war were shot to death.

A Confederate Major was finally captured and ordered executed. Major Enoch Wolf pleaded with Rosecrans to ask Sterling Price to send Tim Reeves, the real perpetrator, to take his place. This went nowhere. The resourceful Major Wolf's Masonic connections carried his protests to the White House. On November 11, 1864, hours before he was to stand before a firing squad, President Abraham Lincoln telegraphed General Rosecrans to "shoot no more men."

The Confederate cause continued to unravel in the next year, but the 15th Missouri Cavalry fought on. Diehard Colonel Reeves led his troops on two skirmishes after Robert E. Lee had surrendered. When he and his men finally gave up at Jacksonport, Arkansas on June 5, 1865, along with other Confederate regiments, Reeves was the only man out of

Tim Reeves' grave is in a small, chain-link fenced plot north of Doniphan. Weathering has almost obliterated the lettering which reads: Col. Timothy Reeves born Apr 28, 1821 Died Mar. 10, 1885. *Separation is our lot. Meeting is our hope.*

829 officers and 8,782 enlisted men, to be denied parole. Charged with the murder of Major Wilson, he was sent to St. Louis. After a time, without explanation, he was released and he returned to Ripley County. Tim Reeves preached and farmed until his death in 1885. His role in the Civil War was not mentioned in his obituary.

After the war, the Irish Wilderness (as everyone now called the area, even though the Irish were gone) became a hideout for lawless bands. These ex-guerrillas did not become front page news like Jesse James. With the governor of Missouri's blessing, the Oregon County Scouts, a militia made up of both ex-Confederates and ex-Union men, was organized "that horse shines and murderers shall be brought to justice." "Devil Dick" Boze whose family had a

Ruins of gristmills of several eras at Boze Spring on the Eleven Point River. The site is only four miles from Hogan's church location and might have been the closest mill operating at that time. Richard "Devil Dick" Boze, its operator, became a feared guerrilla during the Civil War. On June 15, 1865, a patrol dispatched from Pilot Knob reportedly killed him at the Widow Huddleston's house on the Eleven Point River. Another version states he was shot while attending a dance at Aunt Peggy Huddleston's and his body was left to rot in Bone Hollow. Still another story states "Devil Dick" was hunted down and executed as an outlaw by an Oregon County militia after the war. Like the architectural ruins of the millrace, the folk history of the Irish Wilderness is layered and ambiguous.

water mill only four miles from Hogan's church was one of the outlaws the posse hunted down and killed.

Depopulated by Major Wilson and his Union troops and infested afterwards by cutthroats, the Irish Wilderness remained a lonely place for some time.

Father Hogan didn't return "to lead back the poor scattered settlers to their humble but ruined homes."

What happened to them?

Given John Hogan's talent as a storyteller, the conclusion to his narrative of the Irish colony is surprising and somewhat disappointing to modern readers. There is a cinematic quality to his writing. As in a good film, his characters are appealing, the setting picturesque, and there is plenty of action and adventure. But what happened in the end? Father Hogan doesn't know. He relies on secondhand reports by Union cavalry soldiers and a generalized summary of the deprecations of the Civil War in southeast Missouri borrowed from *Campbell's Gazetteer.*

In life as well as art, the public desires resolution. Journalists as well as movie makers understand these pressures to wrap up events in a satisfactory conclusion. Honest reporters like Don Cullimore resist tying things up too neatly. In a seminal, twelve-part series on the Irish Wilderness appearing in the December 1951 and January 1952 issues of the *St. Louis Post-Dispatch*, Cullimore refuted popular melodramatic theories of the vanished colony:

> The disappearance of the Irish often is spoken of as a mystery in the Big Springs country. There is one legend of a massacre of the Irish, but for this there is not only no historical support but convincing evidence to the contrary. There is another legend that the Irish vanished overnight—lock, stock and barrel—in a mass flight from the harassment to which they were subjected. Actually, it appears that neither version has any basis in fact. The situation seems to be that they drifted away, family by family, as repeated pillaging and impressments of the menfolk into military service of one side or the other made their homes no longer tenable. They went to unknown places. As a colony they were scattered beyond recall.

A little southeast of the hamlet of Ponder (called Mill Creek in the mid-1800s) is the old St. Benedict's Catholic Cemetery. There the headstones of Dominick Moran, John Dunne and Martin Timlin read "born in Ireland." All three show up in Bureau of Land Management records as purchasers of land somewhat farther north. Local historians believe that some settlement Irish came back after the war, relocating within the Fourche Creek (Mill Creek) watershed near present-day Ponder.

On a Cram's 1875 Missouri map is the enigmatic toponym, New Ireland. Near the present day site of Handy, this area had a heavy concentration of 1859 and 1860 land patents with Irish claimants. No historical society has any documentation or record of New Ireland as a Missouri place name.

(right) The country where the Griffins settled is relatively level. It is still inhabited today unlike the Irish claims in the hilly country which are largely in Mark Twain National Forest tracts.

Except for Billy Griffin. At least he was the only returnee Don Cullimore could find any record of. Billy's father, Patrick Griffin, was one of the ten applicants for land along Ten Mile Creek that had been denied. On his behalf, Hogan reapplied and Griffin did get his name on a 320 acre parcel of government land deeper in the wilderness where today lies the hamlet of Handy. Irish names are recorded on the rolls of Reeves's militia, but young Billy apparently was the only member of Hogan's colony to enlist in the regular Confederate Army. After serving with General Marmaduke for the war's duration, he was mustered out at Batesville Arkansas and returned to his family's homestead in northwest Ripley County. He was twenty years old. His parents had somehow survived the war on their property, but barely. After relocating them to the more settled

A number of Irish colonists purchased government land in the Barren Forks watershed. Most of that area is now National Forest and structures like this small, well-maintained Baptist church are uncommon. Billy Griffin donated property in the Barren Forks community for a church, but it is not known if this is the site.

environs of Ironton, Billy returned to the wilderness. Several years later he married a widow, Mary Ann Snyder, and adopted her children. Billy Griffin died in 1918; a year later his wife died. The St. Louis newspaperman was able to locate descendants and from interviews learned:

> He was known as Uncle Billy to the entire community. He served three terms as Carter County surveyor, a term as county judge. Father Hogan's dream of an Irish settlement had come to naught, but the record of personal achievement and neighborhood respect Billy Griffin attained is indicative of how the priest's hopes might have been fulfilled had the Civil War not intervened.

Cullimore quoted from Billy Griffin's obituary in the *Current*

Local newspaper of Van Buren: "When a church was organized in the Big Barren neighborhood, "Uncle Billy" was asked to deed a plot of ground as a site for the meeting house. He gave the deed at once, making a proviso that the church might be used by a minister of any denomination."

But was Billy the only Irish colonist to return to the region after the war? Alton resident, Mike Crawford, in his self-published book, *Father Hogan's 1859 Irish Wilderness Settlement*, speculated that while most colonists were driven from their property by the war, there were other Irish who returned:

> So here goes my theory. Remember Patrick Griffin wandering about the region broke? It appears that a great number of the Irish people that moved into the area early on were in bad financial shape. They could not afford any land or the land had already been taken. On the land donated by Fox, Feehan and Madigan, there are a number of old home sites that I am sure were used by the above mentioned people. No doubt, after their homes were destroyed, many of the survivors were taken in by other people in the county. They probably had children and needed help. After the war, with the help of their new friends, they stayed in the country and started a new life. From my research it seems a good number of them settled in the Gatewood community.

Crawford doesn't identify any of these survivors. But his hunch that some of the lost colony persisted in the Gatewood community (then called Mill Creek) bears looking into. In the hamlet of Ponder, six miles west of Gatewood, there is an old Catholic cemetery with grave markers inscribed "Born in Ireland" and dates that would not exclude them from being part of Hogan's settlement. Dominick Moran, whose headstone can be seen on page one, had an 1859 land patent for property in northwest Ripley County, well within Hogan's principal area of settlement. Perhaps he and other members of the colony relocated to the somewhat better farming properties after the War.

If at times undocumented, Crawford's early 1990s treatise on the Irish Wilderness contains promising leads. Looking up deeds in the courthouse records of Oregon and Ripley counties, he compiled a list of Irish names that could have been participants in the colony. Of the thousands of acres

To Frank Drew Esq.
PAT MALLOY,
Originally sung with Immense Success by
In his inimitable Character of The Irish Emigrant,
MR. DAN BRYANT,
at Wallack's Theatre.
PAT MALLOY
IRISH KILKENNY
Words by Dion Boucicault
Arranged by John P. Cook
NEW YORK
Published by Wm. A. POND & Co. 547 Broadway.

There are relatively few written accounts from the perspective of Famine Irish. Our conception of Irish immigrants often comes from popular culture, not from history. Educated observers, even those as sympathetic as Hogan, rarely described their state of mind. Sentimental sheet music like this 1865 song may have overemphasized their feelings of haplessness. Participants in the Ozarks Irish colony certainly had more resolve than poor Pat Malloy who, after journeying to England and America, returned home. *"Me pockets they are empty, but me heart is fill'd wid joy: For ould Ireland is me country, and me name is Pat Malloy."* The Irish Wilderness experience shows that many Irish settlers were willing to take great risks in order to succeed in the New World.

of land entered by persons with Celtic sounding names, Mike Crawford found records of only one colonist who sold their property after the war. Ellen Madigan, widow of Patrick Madigan, sold 320 acres in 1868 for $500. At that time she lived in Indiana. Like a number of the immigrants she was illiterate and signed the contract with her mark.

But the vast majority of their substantial holdings of government land scattered over four, perhaps five, counties were abandoned. In the intervening years, a few of the better agricultural sites were sold at public auction for back taxes. Some of the heavily forested tracts were bought up by speculators. Such rough timbered terrain would be logged out several decades later and again abandoned. Ultimately much of the Irish settlement territory would become national forest. No doubt as courthouse documents are systematically researched and government records become available on the Internet these gaps in the Irish Wilderness saga will be better understood. Someone intrigued by the tale and practiced in genealogical detective work may be able to answer many, if not all, of the questions about the colony's disappearance and what became of its refugees.

Even without the research tools now available, Don Cullimore in 1949 and '50 believed the disappearance of the colony could be explained. Other questions arise however that neither he nor other investigators have addressed. What did the newly arrived Irish think about becoming pioneers in a wilderness they would share with bears, wolves, mountain lions and rattlesnakes? Where did the money come from? Were there other forces behind this ambitious and innovative enterprise to transplant poor Irish immigrants onto land they would own and develop? The founding of the Irish Wilderness may be as great as mystery as its disappearance.

There are no known letters or diaries left by the immigrants. In his book Hogan doesn't address the personal aspirations of his flock. Some clues to their state of mind can be extrapolated from an obscure book published in 1852. Reverend John O'Hanlon's *The Irish Immigrant's Guide for the United States* evaluates the pitfalls and prospects of life in the New World from the perspective of the Catholic clergy of that day. Like Hogan, O'Hanlon was ordained a priest in St. Louis after coming to America a decade earlier. Though Hogan doesn't name him, O'Hanlon was the professor at the Theological Seminary at Carondelet who warned young Hogan of the dire consequences of being anti-slavery in antebellum Missouri. Nowhere does John Hogan mention the *Immigrant's Guide*, but it seems likely that both he and Archbishop Kenrick were familiar with it. Kenrick and O'Hanlon often rode together in a buggy out to the seminary at Carondelet. As one might expect there are warnings in O'Hanlon's guide—watch out for flimflam artists and don't drink too much. It also has passages about the benefits of land ownership and agriculture that offer insights into the Church's motivation to encourage the Ozark colony. O'Hanlon tried to dissuade immigrants from flocking to urban areas where they overloaded the labor pool and drove down wages. He acknowledges at the same time convivial Celts may find country life lonely:

St. Patrick's, "The Rock Church," of Armagh, Missouri. In the early 1840s, Archbishop Kenrick directed the organization of a parish to serve mostly Irish Catholic settlers along the Meramec River in Franklin County, forty miles from St. Louis. Both Fathers John O'Hanlon and James Fox, mentors of Hogan, ministered there; it is likely Hogan was aware of its viability. Descendants of the original Irish settlers still live and farm in the area and maintain the 1850s church and cemetery; three annual festivals are well attended by the entire community.

The tendency of the Irish to crowd into cities or be engaged together in large bodies on public works has already been remarked; and we believe it will be generally acknowledged, that the country must be the proper sphere for the exertions of the agricultural immigrant. Solitude or want of his accustomed society may at first appear irksome, but habit will soon reconcile him to it, and even render it agreeable ... no portion even of the most newly-settled country will present the gloom and desolation his imagination represents.

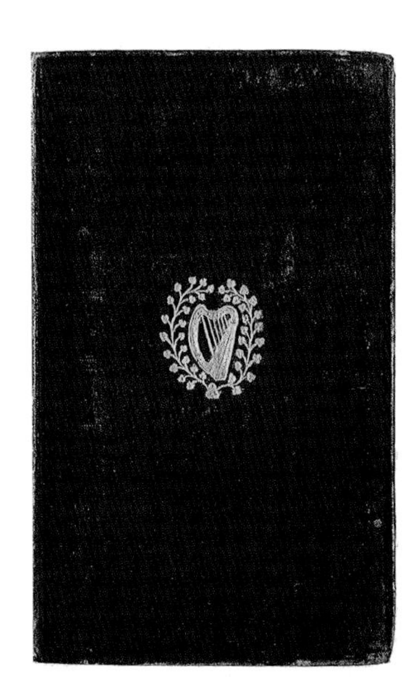

Although Father O'Hanlon, like Pat Malloy, returned to the land of his birth, his writings about how to assimilate immigrant Irish into American culture may have influenced Father Hogan. In *Life and Scenery in Missouri* (above) an 1890s book of his 1850s articles published in *The American Celt* he wrote: *When Catholics meditate removal to a remote and partially settled country, we would advise the formation of companies and colonies; not so much for the purposes of mutual protection and assistance in encountering the dangers of the wilderness, ... as to obtain for themselves that spiritual succor they require.* Courtesy Springfield-Greene County Library.

In Chapter X, Father O'Hanlon alternates passages on the specifics of buying government land and erecting a log cabin with glowing words on the moral and economic benefits of farm life. O'Hanlon's promotional tone creates the suspicion that his readership might be resistant to his recommendations of a bucolic lifestyle. Edward J. Maguire, in the introduction to a 1976 reprint of O'Hanlon's guide, confirms this:

> The vast majority of the Irish immigrants avoided agriculture in America in spite of their rural backgrounds. As a matter of fact it was partly because of their rural backgrounds that they refused to farm. The distress and poverty associated with their previous experience as farmers was enough to discourage a good portion. Others simply preferred the comparatively high wages offered in industry. Even a small amount of money in a weekly pay envelope compares favorably with none at all. Then, too, it should be remembered that transportation to the West, the buying of a farm, and the necessary equipment, seed, or stock cost money that few of the Irish had.

Father Hogan doesn't disclose the financials of the settlement in *On the Mission in Missouri.* There are notations in his handwritten notebook that lead us to believe that he not only located the land and applied for title, he was footing the bill for practically everything. Where did this money come from? *The Catholic Encyclopedia* informs us that when Peter Richard Kenrick became a bishop of St. Louis in 1843 (and soon Archbishop), he inherited a diocese with problems.

> It was no sinecure, for the financial affairs of the Church in St. Louis were in a deplorable condition. There was a very heavy debt on the Cathedral, and he found the Catholics of the diocese by no means anxious to remove it. The bishop then saw that he must either resign or get other means of raising funds, and he took the bold course of getting into the real-estate business. He was most successful. A local gentleman named Thornton made a bequest of 300,000 dollars to the Church; others deposited their money with the bishop; he made fortunate investments in real estate; and, when values generally declined on the outbreak of the Civil War, he paid all his depositors in gold.

Citing his health, John O'Hanlon returned to Ireland in

1854, where he would remain. In 1890 he published *Life and Scenery in Missouri: Reminiscences of a Missionary Priest*, a collection of magazine pieces that originally ran during his American days in *The American Celt*. Dedicated to Peter Richard Kenrick, Father O'Hanlon explained how "the Archbishop's bank" advanced the Catholic faith:

> The money received was borrowed largely by priests and religious with mortgages secured from the different churches and institutions. ... However, when the disturbed state of society and of business set in to St. Louis, consequent on the Confederate Rebellion, the Archbishop desired to wind up the affairs of his Bank, and thus to relieve himself from further monetary responsibility. This plan ... succeeded in a most satisfactory way, and the Archbishop's financial transactions in banking happily came to an end.

Even before the turbulence of the Civil War, Hogan's colony may have begun to unravel. John Joseph Hogan wrote that the year 1860 had been "from beginning to end a year of tremendous excitement and inauspicious portent." During that tumult and before closing his bank, the astute Kenrick would likely have curtailed loaning money to priests. Not only was Father Hogan overcommitted in north Missouri and unable to find other priests to visit his southern mission, his principal source of funding likely dried up. That may explain his absence from the settlement a full year before the war actually broke out. Apparently Kenrick's bank recovered somewhat later in the war years, but by that time the colony's status was unknown. In 1869 the "Bishop's Bank" had become problematic and, though solvent, was closed.

John O'Hanlon's generalizations about the disinclination of the Irish to take up agriculture in the new world were contradicted by a number of Hogan's colonists who apparently took up arms with the locals to fight the Yankees. Misguided perhaps, but indicative that they intended to stay in good standing in their new community and fight and die for their new hill farms if need be. No doubt some did.

What exactly happened long ago in the Irish Wilderness may not be an authentic mystery. Yet the events are both obscure and intriguing enough to continue to evoke curiosity.

Found in the St. Louis Archdiocese Archives are receipts, letters, warranty deeds, and affidavits for actual settlement and cultivation containing the following names. Though this small file of documents relating to the southern colony is fragmentary and incomplete it is probable these individuals were actual settlers or participants in some manner. The X indicates illiteracy.

The abundance of distinct Irish names on 1858-1860 land claims solves the mystery of how the region was named. To the early settlers, who were primarily old American stock, the sudden appearance of foreigners who spoke English with a distinct brogue or were fluent only in Gaelic must have been astonishing. The place name Irish Wilderness has commemorated that long ago culture shock.

NAMES OF COLONISTS IN HOGAN PAPERS

Denis Ahern
William Balcher (?)
John Behair (Behan?)
James Bohan (sp?)
Michael (X) Breman
John Breman
William Bulger (Belcher?)
William Bulger (sp?)
James Burke
Michael Burke
Maurice Byrnes (Burns ? Byrn?)
Honora Calaghan
C_____ Campbell
Patrick Carter
James (Jas or Jos) Casey
Michl Casey
Michael Cavanaugh
Patrick Clifford
Timothy Clifford
Danl Coleman
Mark (X) Connelly
William Connolly
Humphrey Connors
Mary Ann Conrad
John Conway
Michael Cooney
Patrick (X) Corcoran
John Crawley
Mark Crawley
John Cummins
Michl Darrigan
Thomas Denny
James Doolan
Mary (X) Dooley
Finton Dooly
James Evans
Michael Farrell
Patrk Finnegan (sp?)
Hugh Fox
James Fox
Patrick Fox
John Gleeson
Patrick Griffin
William Griffin
James Hammond
Patrick Hammond
Bartholemew Hanley
Catherine (X) Hanley
William Hanrahan
Richard Hartnett
James Hayes
Michael (X) Hogan (sp?)
Jeremiah (X) Hough
Dennis Hurley
William Hyde
James Kelly
Matthew Kilcomon (sp?)
Edward Knox
Michl Leane
Cornelious Malrony
Michael Mara
William McCormick
Thomas McCudden
Jos. Edward McDonough
Jno McHenry
____ McLaughlin
Stephen McNamara
Patrick Mullen, (Mullins?)
Thomas Mulvehille
Jeremiah Murray
Jno Myers
Jno C. Nolan
Peter Nolan
Maurice O'Brien
Letitia O'Conner
Denis O'Sullivan
Peter Quinn
James Rowe
Mary (X) Ryan
Richard Sanford
Louis (X) Schwaelb, (sp?)
Michael Shea
Dennis Sullivan
Mary Sullivan
John Thompson
Michl Walsh
Anthony White
Rush Whitney

In *Father Hogan's 1859 Irish Wilderness Settlement*, Mike Crawford lists names he thought sounded Irish that he found in 1858 and 1859 Oregon and Ripley County courthouse records. A search of the online database of the Bureau of Land Management confirmed many of these individuals did indeed secure land patents in the region from the Jackson Land Office during the years of the colony's founding. Some of the names don't necessarily sound Irish, but then a few of the individuals in the Hogan papers don't either. Searching the BLM records section by section, incidentally, reveals other Irish names like Pat Mulloy, Michael Noonan, and Timothy O'Leary that are not on either list.

POSSIBLE OREGON COUNTY COLONISTS—CRAWFORD

Charles Arnold
Horace Beach
Francis Behan
Isaac Behan, Jr.
S. S. Brainard
Samuel Brashears
Michael Brown
James Byanrs
Patrick Carter
Daniel Clarey
Michael Coffer
Samuel Colt
Thomas Dean
William Dean
Henry Dobson
Patrick Dowel
Robert Downey
Paul Dumphy
Peter Duncan
Patrick Dunn
Joseph Farris
Patrick Feehan
Hasting Feltenburg
James Flannigan
John Fleming
James Flinn
Bernard Flinn
James Forbes
James Fox
Peter Freeman
James Gilbert
Michael Glen
Counoley Hannahan
John Holmes
Jacob House
Constant How
L.P. Hulburd
Edmund Hunley
Edward Hunter
Patrick Hunter
Adolph Isaacs
Charles Johnson
John Kearney
Raphael Keilen
Thomas Kelley
William King
Patt King
Caleb King
Samuel Kintley
Augustus Knox
Bridget Lawless
Edward Lever
Amos Loveland
Patrick Madigan
William Mahon
John McCormick
Henry McHenry
Patrick McMahan
Ann McMahon
Thomas McMahon
Thomas McNamara
Patrick McOwen
John Mitchell
Thomas Moran
John Moran
Dominick Moran
Morris Moses
Patrick Mullins
Thomas Murphy
Richard Murphy
Patrick Murrey
James O'Bryen
Thomas O'Larkin
L.G. Power
Daniel Quinn
Peter Quinn
George Rice
Harmon Richard
Alex Rippy
James Rothrock
Thomas Sappington
William Scott
John Spooner
Dennis Sullivan
Timothy Sullivan
John Sullivan
Yanker Sullivan
John Thornton
Patrick Tobin
Peter Toolr

As Father Hogan noted, "many made land entries at random and without any attempt at selection or examination." Much of the officially designated, 1984 Irish Wilderness includes such agriculturally unsuited claims but Hogan did locate some level tracts. Many of the squares of open land around Handy (2) and Hogan's church site (6) seen on this Landsat satellite photograph were probably cleared by Hogan's Irish colonists. Today they are privately owned pastures surrounded by rougher lands, mostly national forest.

Landsat satellite photograph (opposite page)

1. J Highway
2. Handy – page 76
3. Wilderness – pages 8, 9
4. Camp Five Trailhead pages 7, 11, 99
5. Rev. Patrick Feehan's claim
6. Hogan's church site – page 47
7. CCC Camp – pages 37, 51
8. White's Creek
9. Bardley
10. View of river hills – page 56
11. View of Eleven Point River page 44
12. Boze Mill – page 73
13. Riverton
14. 160 Highway

William Trusdail
Mary Trusdail
Edward Tuohy
Michael Walsh
Thomas Walsh
Bernard William

POSSIBLE RIPLEY COUNTY COLONISTS—CRAWFORD

Charles Bayha
Martin Behan
Patrick Benson
Patrick Clunan
Michael Cooney
James Crowell
Michael Daley
Martin Dally
Thomas Daly
Mennifred Donaghue
Jason Donahan
Patrick Doosy
Patrick Doudall
James Duffey
Luke Duffey
Martin Fimlin
Michael Finley
Patrick Finn
Michael Fitsgerald
Peter Flint
Hugh Fox
John Fox
Patrick Griffin
Thomas Griffin
Edward Heckey
Patrick Hough
John Joyce
James Keily
Samuel Kellum
Michael Lehy
David Lillis
Thomas McAremey
John McAren
Robert McClan
Peter McClanhan
Moses McClure
Jas. McClure
George McClurg
Michael McCoffen
William McCord
Robert McCraw
Edward McDavitt
James McDonald
John McGarrey
Timothy McGlynn
Patrick McGrath
Phillip McGuire
James McKinney
Francis McKinney
William McLaughlin
George McMullin
Thomas McVicker
Henry Monroe
Patrick Moran
James Moran
Patrick Mulley
Bryan Mulligan
Thomas Mulligan
John Murphy
Patrick Nolan
Mark Nolan
Denis O'Brian
Daniel O'Brien
Michael O'Brien
Patrick O'Brien
James O'Bryan
John O'Bryan
Patrick O'Conner
John O'Conner
Thomas O'Donnel
John O'Grady
Patrick O'Kelley
Hughen O'Kennon
James O'Neal
William Quintan
Patrick Rowan
Patrick Ryan
Michael Ryan
Charles St. Clair
Samuel Truesdail
Patrick Walsh
Patrick Ward

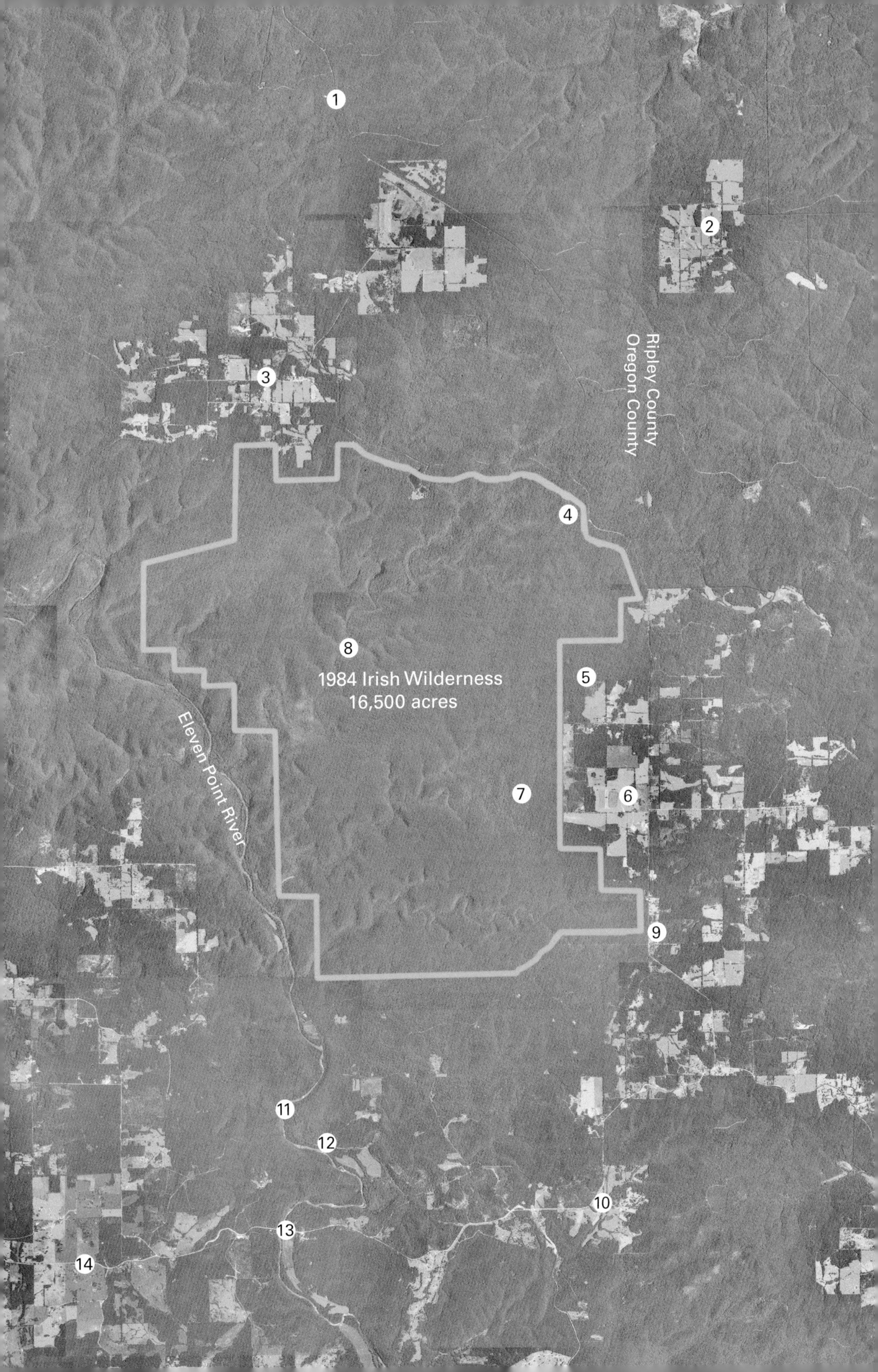
1
2
Ripley County
Oregon County
3
4
8
1984 Irish Wilderness
16,500 acres
5
Eleven Point River
7
6
9
11
12
10
13
14

Father Hogan's Irish settlement was scattered throughout at least four counties in the southeast Missouri Ozarks. This map shows both documented and possible Irish land purchases between the Eleven Point and Current rivers in Oregon and Ripley counties, the areas of most concentrated settlement. The color overlays indicate some Irish ownership within that section (640 acres, or one mile square). Most patents were for the 320 acre maximum allowed by law for one person. Many sections have non-Irish ownership as well. Around the church site, many whole sections were completely taken by members of Hogan's colony.

Mark Twain Forest lands. When the federal government reacquired tax-delinquent, cut-over forests and failed farms in the Ozarks, the Irish Wilderness was a prime candidate.

Land documented in Hogan papers. Though the records are far from complete, the St. Louis Archdiocese Archives contain names almost certainly in some way part of Hogan's settlement. Many of the names on page 84 from these documents are in Carter and Shannon counties, north of the region illustrated in this map of Oregon and Ripley counties.

In his book, *Father Hogan's 1859 Irish Wilderness Settlement*, Mike Crawford speculated this land might be part of Hogan's colony.

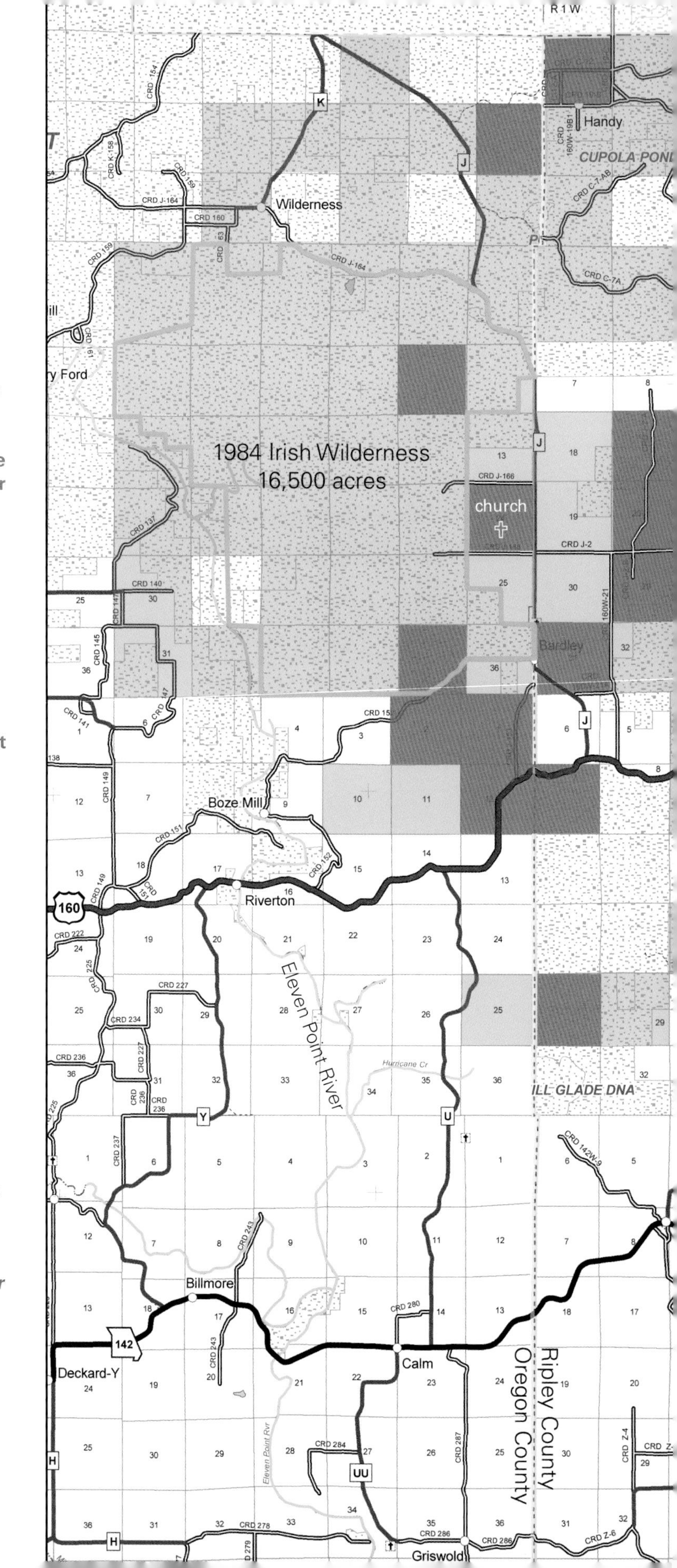

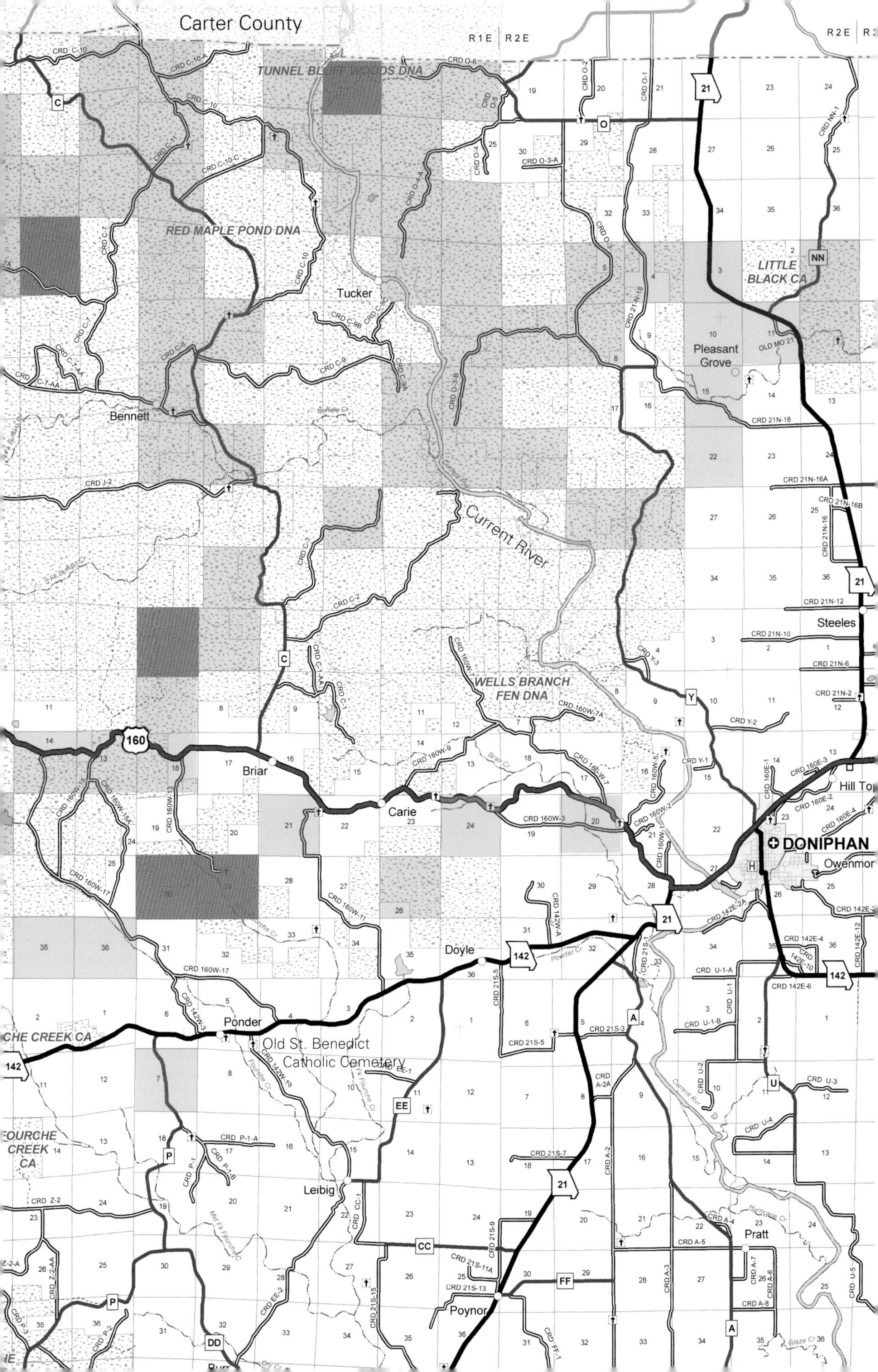

Carter County
R1E
R2E
TUNNEL BLUFF WOODS DNA
RED MAPLE POND DNA
Tucker
Bennett
LITTLE BLACK CA
Pleasant Grove
Current River
Steeles
WELLS BRANCH FEN DNA
Briar
Carie
Hill To
DONIPHAN
Owenmor
Doyle
Ponder
Old St. Benedict Catholic Cemetery
CHE CREEK CA
FOURCHE CREEK CA
Leibig
Pratt
Poynor

PARADISE: LOST, REPOSSESSED AND REGAINED

Frontier conditions persisted for several decades after the Civil War in the land between the Eleven Point and Current rivers. The Irish settlers had vanished (with possibly a few exceptions) but this considerable area was still called the Irish Wilderness. Outlawry subsided and gradually people filtered back in. As John Joseph Hogan had observed when looking for land for the poor Irish immigrants, this country "afforded good advantages for settlement to people of small means and patient, frugal, industrious habits." For those content with food, clothing, shelter, tools, furniture and entertainment that they grew, hunted or made themselves, it was paradise for a time.

The 28-foot iron overshot wheel that once powered Turner Mill is now a photo prop for canoers floating the Eleven Point National Scenic Riverway. Scattered through the surrounding young woods are foundations of stores and houses from the hamlet of Surprise. When the Forest Service acquired the property in 1968, they removed all signs of human occupation except the immovable gigantic mill wheel and a one room schoolhouse on the National Register of Historic Places.

Surrounding the small enclaves of these snake-fenced homesteads were vast forests of mature black and white oaks and shortleaf pine. Father Hogan had commented on the abundance of "timber for fuel, fencing and building purposes." He also noted the "abundance of valuable pine forest."

Well-heeled gentlemen in beaver hats began eyeing this "valuable pine forest" as the American economy began a dramatic postwar expansion. In the May 9, 1903 issue of *American Lumberman* magazine, the "Great Story Of A Great Enterprise" and the "Many Men Of Brain And Brawn" who fulfilled the need for pine lumber is told.

In 1859, the year Father Hogan built his log church in the Ozark wilderness, Elijah Bishop Grandin was poking holes in Pennsylvania shale looking for oil. Although he didn't become as rich as Rockefeller, by 1871 E. B. Grandin was moneyed and looking for more.

The extraction of yellow pine from the southeast Ozarks was accomplished by the big lumber companies with industrial efficiency. By 1940, when this photo was taken, only a mile-long, 200-foot strip on each side of Highway 19 in Shannon County remained uncut. Originally purchased by the Highway Department, this small virgin stand is now one of the L-A-D Foundation's natural areas. Old timers said these ridgetop 200 year old pines were far from the biggest.

That year, Grandin heard rumors about the pine forests of southeast Missouri. Accompanied by his father-in-law, O. H. P. Williams, a Pittsburgh lumberman, he took the train from Pennsylvania to Ironton, still the terminus of the Iron Mountain Railroad. The two rented a team and made "a circuit of about 160 miles seeing a large part of that magnificent belt of timber which eight or nine years later became the property of the Missouri Lumber & Mining Company."

In 1878, E. B. Williams proposed to Grandin that they form a company to exploit Ozark pine resources. Grandin asked twenty-four-year-old John Barber White to accompany Williams and to make a detailed survey of the region. White had financed a sawmill and lumberyard with the Grandins' bank and displayed laudable business acumen. As the *American Lumberman* forty-seven page article (or advertisement, as White paid the magazine $100 a page) explained:

> It was Mr. Grandin who first journeyed into that southwestern wilderness in which civilization has since steadily advanced and will advance for centuries. It was he who found and put into that wilderness J. B. White to work out his plans and to found a commercial commonwealth.

With a few of his Tidioute, Pennsylvania friends, mostly oilmen, the Missouri Lumber & Mining Company was incorporated in 1880. Large tracts were acquired from speculators. Land abandoned by the Irish colonists and many others, could be had for twelve-and-a-half to twenty-five cents an acre at sheriffs' tax auctions on the steps of recently rebuilt county courthouses. Young White was put in charge of the operation and allowed to buy stock on credit The eastern investors' first mill proved too small and was ten miles from a railhead. In an unusually hyperbole-free passage from the 1903 article, the solution is described:

> The new mill was built at Grandin, Mo., ten miles southwest of the small mill, and the contract was made with Gen. George H. Nettleton, president of the Kansas City Southern, and the Kansas City, Ft. Scott & Memphis Railroad, to build a branch railroad eighty-one miles easterly from Willow Spring, Mo., to reach the new mill site and the new town of Grandin. This mill was built in 1887 and 1888 at a small, deep spring lake, a

J.B. White, Jahu Hunter and three members of the Grandin family pose in the Missouri Land and Lumber Company yard at Grandin, Missouri. These Pennsylvania oil and lumber barons were instrumental in transforming the "valuable pine forests" Hogan had observed two decades earlier into dimension lumber, much of which was used to build Kansas City. Courtesy the Special Collections and Archives Dwayne G. Meyer Library, Missouri State University.

valuable natural mill site in the heart of the great pinery.

Interestingly, the lot for Father Hogan's church in Chillicothe (1857) was surveyed by George Nettleton, then a division engineer on the construction of the Hannibal and St. Joseph railroad. John Hogan counted George Nettleton among the "best and noblest of all my friends" throughout his life. When Nettleton's eighty-one mile branch, now called The Current River Railroad, was completed, the Missouri Lumber & Mining Company had access to valuable markets in Missouri, Kansas, Nebraska, and Indian Territory (Oklahoma) as well as the eastern U. S. This encouraged the Pennsylvania investors to increase the capital stock to $500,000. By 1894, the new sawmill ran night and day, producing a daily average of 180,000 board feet, and was said to be the largest in the United States.

Every business in Grandin, except a barber shop and an undertaker, was owned by the corporation. All but the hotel turned a profit. When important customers came to tour the facilities they stayed free of charge. After the obligatory tour, the guests would be taken on float and fishing trips on the Current River, providing the river wasn't full of logs that were periodically floated downstream to be sawed.

Most employees came from out of state. Many had experience in the northern white pine mills. Some locals worked in the woods, but usually on a contract basis. Miss Lillian Loveland, a city girl who worked at Grandin as J. B

White's personal secretary for two years wrote, "The native Missourians—the bushwhackers—were like the poor white trash one reads about."

Had Hogan's immigrants somehow endured the war, it's likely many would have been hired. The company built Catholic, Baptist, Methodist and Congregational churches for the workers. Unattended, the Catholic church became the library.

There were several other well-funded concerns cutting the virgin Ozark yellow pines. Grandin had learned the value of cooperation between competitors in the Pennsylvania oil patch. In 1897, the Missouri Lumber & Land Exchange was formed with offices in Kansas City to "stabilize" (i.e. fix) lumber prices. By 1903, the three largest Ozark mills and three largest Louisiana mills (all owned by stockholders of the Missouri firms) may not have been a monopoly, but they were big enough to raise the price of pine lumber—in one year as much as ten times. Profits were spectacular. By 1904, Missouri Lumber & Mining Company had made over $2 million. In 1907, the monthly stockholders' dividend was $60,000, an impressive return on a $500,000 investment.

Another member of the Exchange capitalized at half a million dollars was the Ozark Land & Lumber Company with a large mill at Winona. It is this company that logged the heart of the Irish Wilderness. J. H. Hahn reported to the *American Lumberman* that "the timber in which the company is now logging is the best it has ever cut." The following passage from the 1903 article confirms the persistence of the legend of Hogan's settlement:

> The company is just about to and in fact is at present operating extensively in the "Irish Wilderness" a locality famous in southern Missouri as the place where many, many years ago a colony of Irish Catholics located with a view to establishing there a great church and settlement. The settlement did not succeed. The wilderness is left and the nationality of the people who had the enterprise at heart gave it its name. It contains some fine timber. This was long before the war. These early settlers had extensive churches, schools and the like.

Widely used locally, the place name "Irish Wilderness" was rare in print until conservationists and journalists picked it up

During the timber boom at the turn of the last century, Hogan could have ridden a train from Kansas City to Camp Five (now the trailhead for the Irish Wilderness) only two miles from the church site. Of course, for the last leg, he would have had to ride an Ozark Land & Lumber Company logging tram. By then, of course, the Irish colony was only a memory. When the pine was cut out in the early 1900s, the Current River Line folded and the region again became relatively inaccessible. Courtesy the Special Collections and Archives Dwayne G. Meyer Library, Missouri State University.

a half a century later.

By the end of World War I, the pine was exhausted. Anticipating this inevitability, several of the big lumber companies had optimistically put 'mining' or 'land' in their names. John Barber White hired prospectors and authorized hundreds of pits and shafts but no mineral deposits of commercial concentration were found. Sales of land were disappointing, too. Model peach and apple orchards had been planted by White. The big companies attempted to convince the public that the cutover woods could be farmed but most of these acreages were unsuited for agriculture.

Ozark taxes were surprisingly high. Cutover forest property was assessed at the same rate as when it had valuable timber. It made business sense to write it off and move on. The counties repossessed much of the rugged southeast Ozarks for the second time.

Moved to the edge of the modern market economy by the timber boom, the area sank back into subsistence living. In some ways times were harder than after the Civil War. Store-bought had replaced homemade; pioneer skills and crafts had been almost forgotten. The old forests, a storehouse of

AMERICAN MATCH & PRTG. CO.• CHICAGO
MADE U.S.A.
CIVILIAN CONSERVATION CORPS • UNITED STATES
SAFETY PAYS
CO. 3751
CCC
CAMP OZARK
BARDLEY, MISSOURI
CLOSE COVER BEFORE STRIKING

Matchbook cover of Civilian Conservation Corps Camp 3751 which was located only a mile west of the site of Father Hogan's log church. Unlike most of Franklin Roosevelt's Depression-era programs, the CCC was popular in the Ozarks. Young men were paid $30 a month ($25 of which was sent home) to restore the cut-over pine forests among other rustic duties that did not compete with union jobs.

raw materials and game, were not the same.

Shortleaf pine did not grow back—at least not in pure stands. Most of the timbered-out areas were colonized by a tangle of young red and black oaks. In a futile attempt to encourage grass to grow for open range the locals burned the woods. Firing the young hardwoods did not have the same effect as periodically burning a forest of large, fire-resistant trees, a management technique practiced by Indians and continued by early settlers.

Burning the cutover forest fired up the emerging conservation movement. A heated national debate had been simmering for years about the depletion of forest resources and game. Urban sportsmen blamed the natives of the region unjustly as the penetration of railroads had facilitated both the timber removal and market hunting.

Professor Conrad Hammar of the University of Missouri criticized "Ozark individualism, a synonym for pioneer institutions" for creating "relief loads in Ozark counties higher than in any of the other rural counties in Missouri." His solution was for Ozarkers to stop burning the woods, move into villages and abandon "the almost child-like faith in private institutions regulated by competition alone and the near abhorrence of government interference in the interests of conservation." His 1935 paper "Institutional Aspects of Ozark Decline" hopefully noted "to date eight National Forest units totaling approximately two million five hundred thousand acres have been established in the Ozarks."

As it was during Franklin Delano Roosevelt's administration that the cutover Ozark woods were federally re-acquired, it is sometimes forgotten that his cousin Teddy began government involvement with forest conservation. Passionate outdoorsman, Theodore Roosevelt, created the National Forest Service in 1905. Passionate, progressive Republican John Barber White was a friend of the first Chief Forester, Gifford Pinchot. White explored the idea of deeding all of his cutover lands back to the United States. This was impossible as the state legislature did not allow federal purchase until the 1930s. White's son, R. B. White, would offer a 3,127 acre fragment of the once vast holdings of the Ozark Land & Mining Company to the National Forest in 1934.

Arguing against the creation of the 16,500 acre Irish Wilderness, locals pointed out that though the area might look virginal the region had long been modified by man's works. Indeed, the ruins of CCC Camp 3751, Camp Bardley, are within the Wilderness boundary.

Republican progressives of the early 1900s were as fond of the "saving for future generations" policy justifications as contemporary government agencies. What they wanted to 'save' were resources for future economic use. Franklin Roosevelt's administration added social and cultural goals to resource management. The impoverished Ozarks had, in the 1930s, a profile that might recommend it for New Deal social engineering—a once Edenic natural landscape despoiled by industrial extraction, exploited underemployed workers and a folk culture wounded by modernity. John Vachon, Farm Security Administration photographer, did snap some Oregon County goat farmers, but overall the Ozarks did not get the attention from FDR's imagists and reformers that the Deep South did—lacking perhaps photogenic soil erosion or oppressed minorities.

If New Deal intervention was less intrusive in the Ozarks than in Dixie, the reappearance of a federal presence was

1532 University Avenue
July 10, 1937

Mr. Robert Marshall
U. S. Forest Service
Washington, D. C.

Dear Bob:

When I visited the "Irish Wilderness" of Missouri in 1929 there was nearly a county of woods substantially roadless.

I have recently seen a map of recently constructed and projected state and federal highways in this area. The largest remaining fragment is 14,000 acres. This is officially labelled as a wilderness area and turkey refuge. I hear it is being fenced.

I need hardly point out to you that aside from the Superior and the Porcupine—whose history I need not recount—this was the only large wild spot in the Upper Mississippi Basin.

There must, of course, be pros and cons in this question which I am unfamiliar with, and cannot easily find out about. Except as a private citizen, it is also none of my business. On the surface, though, it looks like another case of chopping up a wild area and then labelling one of the chips a wilderness.

I don't want to burden you, or Lyle Watts, with a report on the question I have raised. I don't even expect a letter. I would, however, like to make sure that somebody with a sympathetic view of all the conflicting interests has given these plans a "once-over" to make sure that the road engineers have not been running wild. I have a special affection for this area, and to an old Service man it is disquieting to feel that conversion into a National Forest or Park always means the esthetic death of a piece of wild country.

Yours sincerely,

Aldo Leopold
Professor of Game Management

vh

Although he was never a member, the Sierra Club called wildlife biologist Aldo Leopold "the father of the American wilderness movement." Leopold had a cabin on the lower Current River and hunted and explored the surrounding country. In a 1926 letter to his wife about his experience caught in an ice storm in the Irish Wilderness, he called it "the wildest remaining spot east of the plains." After his 1937 letter (left) to the influential Bob Marshall, the area that would become part of the wilderness system forty-seven years later was singled out for minimal logging and road construction by the Forest Service. Letter courtesy Aldo Leopold Papers, University of Wisconsin Archives.

only slightly less welcome than were Union troops in the Civil War. Conservation was the battle flag the invading feds carried this time around. Telling a man what he can kill and when and interfering with the God-given right to set fire to the woods were unacceptable to many natives. These 'furriners' were supported by some Missouri groups as well. The state had reorganized and depoliticized its Department of Conservation in 1937. It worked hand-in-glove with the federal government implementing Roosevelt-era programs. Among other things, the new agency learned the value of outreach. Since the 1940s, their magazine has been promoting up-to-date conservation concepts employing idealized nature photography, cartooned baby animals, and lively, professionally written features.

In the July 1948 *Missouri Conservationist* is an article by Edgar Allen titled "Current River—Descendant of Springs." In his coverage of the lower Current River, the author mentions "an abortive attempt to colonize the region before the Civil War with Irish laborers who had been working on a railroad."

> And just to the west of the river's lower stretch lies the Irish Wilderness, a half-fabulous area where few people live and the roads are mostly forest trails. From the Wilderness still

Where to go
... in the
OZARKS
By KEITH McCANSE
50¢
1931
FOURTH
ANNUAL
EDITION
OVER TWELVE HUNDRED PLACES
TO FISH - CAMP - TOUR - PLAY - REST

Listed in Keith McCanse's 1931 *Where to Go in the Ozarks* travel guide, the still-primitive country that Hogan's colony had occupied seventy years earlier was described as one of the "twelve hundred places to fish – camp – tour – play – rest".
IRISH WILDERNESS.—In Oregon and Shannon counties north and east of Eleven-Point River is perhaps the greatest extent of wild and uncultivated territory in the Missouri Ozarks. This is one spot where the wild deer of Missouri made their last stand, and are now being brought back in satisfactory quantities.

> come tales of panthers and bears—though none have been verified—and the rugged terrain is unsafe for tenderfeet who do not know the country. It is easy to get lost here.

Three years later, Dan Saults, the *Conservationist* editor, and Don Wooldridge, its photographer, published a five-page article, "The Irish Wilderness." Saults begins with a poetic evocation:

> Like Shangri-La Fiddler's Green and the Ozark region of which it is a part, the Irish Wilderness is a state of mind. Its boundaries are where one chooses to say they are, its present history is compound of legend and half-fact. Furthermore, it is a place of dreams and fancy; its tree-shrouded hollows are receptacles for tales of the hills. It exists, to most people, as a name that tickles the fancy and stimulates the imagination.

> Even to one who stands in the region and touches the oaks that have replaced much of the virgin pine that covered it, the Irish Wilderness is still a state of mind. It can seem a remote, incredible land still haunted by leprechauns and Anglo-Saxon ghosts; or it can be an example of an area that was exploited for its timber, ravaged and cast away, and is now making a comeback; or it can be a dreary, barren, sparsely inhabited divide between the Eleven Points and Current rivers.

Nicely written in local color style, the piece blends history, travel and a conservationist message—the land "has been betrayed by man, and is now being healed." Don Cullimore, a St. Louis newspaperman, drove over the rough roads in his station wagon with Saults, Wooldridge, and their local guide, E.R. Burrows, step-grandson to colony survivor Billy Griffin.

In the December 31, 1951 *St. Louis Post-Dispatch*, the first of Cullimore's twelve articles on the Irish Wilderness appeared. From the first of the series ("Writers Ignored Irish Wilderness Area of S. Missouri Despite Dramatic History") to the last ("Residents Fighting to Keep Army Engineers From Damming Rivers, Flooding Major Scenic Attractions, Farmland"), they were also well crafted, conveying a then-and-now sense of place. Although frustrated by the state's two historical societies' lack of information on the settlement, he and Saults had obviously located a copy of John Joseph Hogan's rare book, *On the Mission in Missouri*. Both liberally quote Hogan.

Eleven Point River floaters during johnboat days sought smallmouth bass. Many canoers today target trout. Below Greer Springs, the water is cold enough to sustain a put-and-take rainbow trout fishery.

The two writers would remain friends throughout long careers. Saults became chief of information for the U. S. Fish and Wildlife Service; Cullimore, after being public relations director for Johnson Outboard Motors, became executive director of the Outdoor Writers Association of America. Both were recipients of that professional association's Legends Award. Thirty years later and retired, both became leaders in the effort to secure official wilderness status for the Irish Wilderness.

When Cullimore and Saults began exploring and writing about the cut-over yet largely forested lands between the Eleven Point and Current rivers, the story of Father

Turner Mill as it appeared in a late 1940s booklet distributed by the Missouri Resources and Development Division. "Time is taking its toll of these old landmarks, once the scene of busy milling activity," reads the nostalgic caption.

Hogan's colony was fading but authentic folklore. Except for Hogan's all but forgotten account in *On the Mission in Missouri* there was little in print about the settlement or the region. While the publicists for the conservation movement acknowledged the motive behind the Catholic colony, they saw the Irish Wilderness as a metaphor for larger land use issues. What, if any, messages were implicit in the folklore of the place remain unknown. Impressed by the novelty and the magnitude of the effort to transplant poor immigrants into the Ozark hills, the log cabin natives seemed to have treated the event as a somewhat melancholy historical and topographic marker. It's unlikely old American oral tradition would have attached moral significance to the subsequent cutting of the forest (Paradise Lost), the formation of national forests (Paradise Repossessed) or the effort to re-grow the trees and reestablish the wildlife (Paradise Regained). That interpretation is from the scripture of pantheism, not Christian culture, formal or folk.

Don Cullimore and Dan Saults were likely unaware of the philosophical, anti-theological origins of Aldo Leopold's branch of conservationism that would evolve into

The spring branch that once powered Turner Mill issues from a cave in a dolomite bluff. Only mossy rockworks and the wheel just downstream indicate that this was once the site of an active gristmill. Eden restored by the U. S. Forest Service.

environmentalism. A fellow World War II officer is in fact quoted in Saults' Outdoor Writers of America bio as being "surprised by his strong belief in the Bible and its literary values." Leopold, co-founder of the Wilderness Society, was not only candid about his pantheistic beliefs, he expressed his feelings that Christianity was complicit in environmental degradation. His son, Luna, stated, "I think he, like many of the rest of us, was kind of pantheistic. The organization of the universe was enough to take the place of God." Estella, his Catholic wife, said, "... his religion came from nature." Judeo-Christian tenets that God made the earth for man's benefit ran counter to Leopold's belief that all life forms were equal. Though the creed that God is nature, and its corollary that wilderness is Eden, doesn't dominate federal government policy, the language of the Wilderness Act of 1969 has a pantheistic ring. Section 2(c) states, "A wilderness, in contrast with those areas where man and his own works dominate the landscape, is hereby recognized as an area where the earth and its community of life are untrammeled by man, where man himself is a visitor who does not remain."

To a great many citizens and certainly all the hardscrabble natives of the Irish Wilderness, such mystical beliefs were

Just off the square in Alton is a mural depicting Oregon County history; in its center is Turner Mill. Only a few remember the actual mill. Fewer still recall the days when the big wheel turned and ground corn into flour. Much Ozark history has gone from fading memories to fading paint.

perplexing and their practical ramifications threatening. Folks living in small frame houses heated by wood burning stoves within scattered acreages surrounded by vast national forest scarcely felt their "own works dominated the landscape." They, like Father Hogan, knew the land was marginal, hardly Paradise. It was and will always be just the Irish Wilderness. "Why enact a bunch of regulations?" Anna Smith, who clerked the still-open Wilderness store, told a *Kansas City Star* reporter, "We resent the outsiders coming in here and telling us what to do with our land."

As the federal law was debated, timbering and mining concerns waved money in front of the residents. If only the preservation efforts would be defeated, these industrial lobbies cynically promised, hundreds of jobs would be created. Saults and Cullimore who had promoted the mystique of the Irish Wilderness for decades, were joined by activists like John Karel in an effective publicity campaign to counter such illusionary economic benefits. Mrs. Smith, the Wilderness shopkeeper, had additional concerns. If "they (the environmentalists) get their way, they'll have nudist colonies, whatever, out there." Truth be told, what the one hundred or so Ozarkers thought didn't matter. Politicians, bureaucrats and urban recreationalists decided

This down-home Mountain Home mural by hometown artist Juanita Bright is now blocked by a wall. Obstacles to a local vision of history are both accidental and systematic. Dominant government cultural interpretations are likely to be more secular and propagate current federal ideologies. In spite of this, Ozarkers perpetuate their version of the past at festivals, in museums, through local histories and on the Internet.

the issue. Twenty years after the Wilderness Act of 1964 was passed, the Irish Wilderness was approved by Congress "in furtherance of the purpose." Occasionally, a canoer will skinny dip in the Eleven Point River, but two decades and counting there are still no nudist colonies in Oregon County.

In spite of the leftist and pantheistic philosophies of some wilderness movement founders, like Marshall and Leopold, preservation is but one of the multi-purpose goals of the U. S. Forest Service. Little has changed. The 16,500 acre part of the larger Irish Wilderness region is today a law on the books, a spot on maps, a key word on Internet search engines and a destination for hikers and trail riders. Many locals hunt turkey and deer there just like they do within other parcels of the vast regenerated mixed oak and pine forest that Father Hogan's immigrants briefly took title to.

THE WILDNESS OF YOUTH

Much about the Irish Wilderness is unknown, perhaps ultimately unknowable. To contemporary readers, its creator and chronicler, John Joseph Hogan, may be something of a cipher as well. His realistic writing style captured the flux of the frontier and the American Civil War. In his pages we feel the humanity of those who lived through those turbulent times. Hogan, the adventurous pioneer priest, is an active character in these stories but he tells them without the self promotion and self justification contemporary readers are accustomed to. John Hogan was not a modernist, but his sparse, objective writing was certainly not effusive Victorian prose either. Rarely is he introspective. Never is he psychological. *Fifty Years Ago: A Memoir* is a richly detailed record of growing up in rural Ireland. That his mother died when he was three years old was not a life changing trauma. He had no power struggle with his father. There was no sibling rivalry between him and his four brothers and two sisters. Only occasionally in *On the Mission in Missouri* did he depart from his carefully crafted transcriptions of the objective world and reflect upon himself:

> And here I may apologize for having given myself, unnecessarily as may have been, to enterprises of responsibility, hardship and danger, no doubt regarded by wiser heads than mine as but the wildness of youth.

North Missouri today provides small opportunity to view the native prairies Father Hogan loved. Photographs of unplowed grasslands in this book were taken on Missouri Prairie Foundation preserved tracts in southwest Missouri.

Puzzling is Father Hogan's silence about the fate of his Irish colony. There is his poignant lament: "Who now will lead back the poor scattered settlers to their humble but ruined homes." Nowhere else does he elaborate on his feelings for the tragic loss of the settlement he worked so diligently to

found. "The Wildness of Youth" passage is sincere but in his writings there is no guilt-ridden confession worthy of a mid-nineteenth century priest. Hogan's emotional response to the destruction of the settlement might be inferred from his story about a small disappointment that happened in 1861.

Father Hogan was asked to perform a wedding in the country. Though friends of the couple to be wed had asked him to travel the day before the ceremony, he was committed to his regular appointment for Mass at Mexico on the third Sunday of the month. The slow train back reached Chillicothe at nearly 2:00 in the morning:

> Soon after daylight, I set out in a two horse sleigh with a driver, for Carroll County. The weather was intensely cold. Deep snow had covered the ground, and it was freezing hard through an azure blue atmosphere, with scarcely perceptible sunshine. We crossed Grand River on the ice, and without risk, as heavily loaded teams had made the frozen river a traveled roadway. Afterwards, driving over the level alluvial lands along the west bank of Shoal Creek, between it and Utica, in going over the slippery surface of a frozen lake, from which the wind had blown away the snow, we noticed that one of the horses was not properly shod for the journey, as he was constantly slipping on the glassy surface. Soon, in spite of all we could do to prevent the accident, that poor horse fell down heavily, and was with great difficulty got to stand up and trust to his feet again. That was the first accident and delay in "the haste to the wedding" which had now or never to be played to time. After a little, the horses were on the move once more, slowly at first, then gradually limbering to the task, a high and steady rate of speed was gained. Having passed Shoal Creek and the frozen lagoons along its banks, the rolling prairies through the Blue Mound country and over the borders into Carroll County were passed in speed and safety, and there seemed no doubt whatever that the marriage rendezvous would be reached in good time. But disappointments will come anon to mar the fullest hopes and cloud the brightest scenes. Some miles farther on, and within one hour's drive of the end of the journey, when near Bogard's Mound, in crossing a wooden bridge without parapets, that spanned a frozen stream, one of the horses affrighted by the loose, shaky planks under his feet, shied badly, and shoved the other horse sidelong over the bridge, with result that one horse and the sleigh were on the bridge, and the other horse was on his back on the

ice below. Having scanned the situation we hastily unhitched the horse on the bridge from the sleigh, and tied him by the halter to a tree near by; then going to the relief of the horse that was down, we found him on-his back, trembling and stunned, his four legs standing out from his body, straight upright. Nothing could induce him to rise, or to make an effort to do so. He suffered himself to be shoved and turned round and round on his back on the ice, his limbs seeming to grow stiffer all the while. At length, when he had rested himself well, and when the fright had left him, he seemed inclined to make efforts to rise. Then, some brambles placed along his sides and around him, he succeeded in rising, and getting on his feet again. Upon examination we found he was uninjured, though somewhat bruised and greatly frightened and stunned. It required considerable time to limber him, and get him ready for work, by rubbing his limbs, and relaxing them by exercise. Then the harness had to be re-adjusted and tied and knotted together. Afterwards, the horses were brought together, and hitched to their traces. The whole loss of time by the accident was fully three hours. Already night had set in. Six miles remained to be traveled, necessarily at a slow gait. The wedding hour had come and gone. And there was no courier near, to be sent forward in speed, to announce the completion of the journey with its reverses. At length we arrived, tired, weary and disheartened. The marriage feast had been partaken of. "The lights were fled, the garlands dead, the banquet hall deserted." The marriage party with the bride and bridegroom had set out in sleighs towards Lexington to have the marriage duly solemnized there. I did my best. It was a great disappointment. But the causes were beyond my control. And now though more than thirty years have elapsed, my heart still beats with pity for them, for having had to go so far through the cold winter's night, for the performance of a sacred duty, the appointed minister of which was near at hand, even at their very doors, if they but knew of his approach. Other reasons, too, there are, why the sadness of that occasion, seems to be a never-ceasing one. The good and beautiful bride of that night, has long since been laid to rest in her quiet grave. And the worthy bridegroom, ever with bowed head, goes down the hill of life, silent and alone; seemingly with no purpose on earth, but to look forward to another marriage feast, and in a better world, where sorrow shall be no more, and all disappointment will have passed away.

"YOU MUST BE BORN AGAIN." St. John 3:7

Weary and tired I endeavored to attend to the duty of reciting my Office and night prayers, in the comfortable but now cheerless house, which the disappointed wedding party had so recently deserted. To seek immediate rest, in my unnerved and over-fatigued condition, would be quite useless. I reposed quietly for a while in an easy chair. The venerable lady of the house, whose daughter was the bride, was too anxious for the safety of the wedding party, then toiling through the snow, to compose herself to sleep. She too, had lulled herself into a wakeful repose, on a rocking chair, before the smouldering embers in the fire-place. The lamps had been turned down to a dull shady gloom. Now and then we conversed a little in under tones, in keeping with the solitariness of the scene and the midnight hour, which a drowsy little timepiece on the mantel had just announced. What sounded like a feeble knock was heard at the door, but there were no voices or footfalls that we could hear. After a while, the faint knock was repeated, and with it a feeble voice asked for admission. The lady of the house arose and went to the door, which, after having listened warily awhile, she cautiously opened. A lady entered, wrapped in heavy winter robes, and bearing an infant sheltered in her bosom. She was attended by her husband, a middle-aged gentleman, likewise dressed in winter clothing, and of respectful demeanor. Having exchanged salutations with the lady of the house, with whom they were acquainted, they asked to be introduced to the priest, saying that they had brought their babe to be baptized, and had come at that late hour, fearing he might be gone, were they to defer the baptism until the morning. Their heroic christian faith was rewarded. Six miles the dear parents had come with their babe in a sleigh, through the piercing storm of frost and snow, that it might be born anew to Christ. At once the lights were relighted and the fires rekindled. A new joy pervaded the whole place. It was happy as a Christmas night. A babe was born again "of water and the Holy Ghost, and made heir with Christ to a Heavenly kingdom." The event, as of record in the parish baptismal register of Chillicothe, is as follows: "1861, January 23rd, I baptized Catharine, born Nov. 4, 1860, daughter of Edmond Shine and Prudence Eccleston, his wife; Sponsor, Paulina Newman. John Hogan." Paulina Newman, the sponsor, was the venerable lady of the household. Her daughter, Miss Newman was the bride of the disappointed wedding. After the

John Hogan appreciated the beauty of the north Missouri tall grass prairies in Indian Summer. He also witnessed these natural meadows in winter traveling alone on horseback, sometimes at night lost in a blizzard. His writings are of landscape experienced, not just looked at. The demise of the Irish colony deprived us of more of Hogan's writing on the nature of the Ozarks which his continued involvement would surely have given us.

> baptism I retired for a short time to rest. Early in the morning, in the midst of a blinding snow-storm, that had fairly obliterated the roads, I set out on the homeward journey, the birds of the air—victims of cold and hunger—falling down and fluttering in death in the snow around me. It was some hours in the night when I arrived at Chillicothe.

"I did my best. It was a great disappointment. But the causes were beyond my control." Father Hogan's disappointment at being unable to perform the wedding was ameliorated by the opportunity to baptize an infant brought to him in the middle of that snowy night. Given the grief he must have felt about the lost colony in the wilderness one must conjecture his quest for redemptive acts was intense and lifelong, but private.

BISHOP HOGAN

From the 1861 story set in the snowscape of north Missouri, John Hogan flashes forward to an 1868 winter. The jump-cut to seven years later and the objective tone and strong visual style seem more stylistically akin to cinema than to conventional nineteenth century autobiography. "One More January Blast" tells of a journey taken alone on horseback to minister to scattered Catholics near the Iowa line. The trip goes well until he rides off late one afternoon for a hamlet that is farther than he realizes:

> The weather was intensely cold, and the ground which was covered with snow, was icy and rough. In a little while I crossed the Thompson Fork of Grand River on the ice, on a trail of straw laid across to prevent cattle from slipping and falling down. Thence my course was East by North, with a freezing blast and small dry snow striking me fast in the face. It was useless that I tried to dodge the cold, by turning my head aside to right or left. I needed to keep a straight onward outlook, to guide my horse safe, over broken roads, ravines and tree stumps that beset my way. The night came on apace, and with it the discouraging thought, that I was still many miles from a certain saw-mill, at which, as had been previously arranged, a guide was to meet me at the hour of sunset. When I had reached the saw-mill, it was three hours past sunset, and no guide was there to lead me on, over roads of which I knew little.

Photogravure portrait of Hogan from the 1889 *Illustrated History of The Catholic Church in the United States*. Bishop Hogan remained a tall, slender, erect figure throughout his life. There is no mention of horseback riding in his later years, but his frequent five and six mile walks were duly noted by reporters.

Thinking the priest "had been deterred by the bad weather from venturing out on the journey" the guide didn't wait. Lost, Hogan barely makes it to a farmhouse past midnight. In the morning he had "bleeding lungs, the first and only attack of the kind in my life." He hears some confessions and

celebrates Mass but cannot preach and has to cut his trip short:

> I was thankful to God for the strength given me to reach home alive, if not in good health. At Chillicothe, whilst resting to regain my wasted strength and energy, I received a strange document written in Latin and in a particular hand which translated into English reads as follows.
>
> RIGHT Reverend Sir: Among many things of advantage to the Catholic religion, that were done by the United States Plenary Council held in Baltimore in 1866, the proposition of the Most Reverend Fathers therein assembled, to erect new episcopal sees for the greater increase of the christian name and the more diligent care of the faithful, is clearly to be recorded. Since therefore one of these new sees is designated to be the city of St. Joseph, in the province of St. Louis, it has pleased our Most Holy Father, with the advice of the Sacred Congregation of the Propaganda, to entrust the government of it to Your Right Reverence, whose doctrine and virtue have been clearly vouched for by trustworthy recommendations. The Holy Father is therefore fully persuaded that you will use all your care and diligence, so that having become a perfect example to the flock, you will so bear the aforesaid episcopal burthen, as to gather and lay up a most abundant harvest in the store-house of Jesus Christ ... At Rome from the Sacred Congregation of the Propagation of the Faith; January 26, 1868.

It is a movie moment. The tall, lanky parish priest has returned with "bleeding lungs" from riding through the harsh Great Plains winter to minister to scattered enclaves of poor farmers and finds he has been selected to become a bishop of the Roman Catholic Church. He is 38 years old. Most of his sixteen years of doing God's work has been spent as a missionary in thinly settled, isolated rural areas. His prairie mission in north Missouri has promise, but like the raw country and the hardscrabble settlers it is a work in progress. Father Hogan's ambitious effort to settle Irish immigrants in the wilderness of the Ozark highlands has failed and the loans have been written off. But this austere and at times dangerous life is what he dreamed of as a child. Pondering the "strange document" he recovers his health and spends the spring back in the saddle visiting Milan, Clarksburg and Unionville. He preaches, gives Communion and baptizes babies. When the Bulls—the official papers—confirming his appointment as bishop arrive from the Vatican in March, he leaves them unopened on his desk. Finally, he breaks the red seal and looking at them questions the wisdom of the whole proposal:

> That I was surprised at what had been done does not at all express what my feelings were. With the greatest respect for the Sacred Congregation of the Propaganda, I could not help seeing, that either it had acted on an important matter without the full information; or that it had placed too great faith in the progressiveness of a backward corner of the state of Missouri, to suppose that it could become even an insignificant diocese in a hundred years.

Hogan does the math for the new diocese and comes up with six hundred families and three thousand souls. "What I found, was, that throughout its whole extent, there were not as many Catholics, as would, if all were together, make one congregation, such as could be easily attended by two priests." Ever the realist, John Hogan goes to St. Joseph to see with his own eyes the Pro-Cathedral:

> The church edifices were of the poorest kind. The largest, the pro-cathedral, was a low, narrow, squalid brick house, built in three different sections, and at three different times. The floor was below the street level, and much of it quite underground. The walls and roof were held together by wooden stanchions bolted outside on the walls, and by hog chains inside, athwart the little building. The site was in a hollow, in the curve of an open sewer or creek; the overflow from which, with every rain, poured mud and muck through the doors and chinky foundations in upon the floor of the rickety structure. Around the church was a dense growth of weeds, shrubs, and low intertangled shade trees; moss-covered from the constant wet of the overflow of the creek, as were likewise the walls of the building. There had been at one time a fence around the church, but it was now a jagged outline of rents and gaps; evidently made so by the assaults of droves of hogs that frequented the place, and that took great delight in ploughing up the soft mold with their long snouts, and rubbing their mucky backs and sides against the church walls, doors, and door posts. The hogs were in possession, and judging by their diligence, the palm was theirs for unequaled church-going qualities. With very subdued, if not altogether crushed feelings,

> I returned to Chillicothe, to meditate upon what further steps I should take.

In "Final Surrender," the last subchapter of *On the Mission in Missouri*, John Joseph Hogan acknowledges "the fearful burden and responsibility of the episcopal office." He recalls how he "undertook against all hope of success, the apparently very foolish task of opening missions in north Missouri, where the odds were against me." He notes the significance that his appointment as bishop is to the newly created See of St. Joseph, his own Confirmation name:

> I received consecration in St. Louis on the feast of the Holy Name of Mary, Sunday, September 13, 1868. The following Sunday devoted to the contemplation of the Sorrows of the Mother of God at the foot of the Cross I was on duty at the pro-Cathedral in St. Joseph.
>
> —FINIS—

There is another version of these events. A sketch of Bishop Hogan's career published in the August 22, 1895 *Kansas City Catholic* has him returning the papers unsigned:

> But the unassuming country priest did not want to be a bishop. He feared the responsibility and did not care for the dignity. Consequently he sent the Bulls back, addressing them to Archbishop Kenrick who was then in Rome. But the Archbishop promptly returned them saying that he was not the person to whom the Bulls should have been sent, at the same time advising Father Hogan to accept. Those who know Bishop Hogan best will readily believe that it was only after much serious thought and much fervent prayer that he finally consented to accept the proffered dignity.

Earlier in that newspaper article we learn that the colony in the wilderness has not been forgotten three decades after its extinction:

> From his experience in the sacred ministry and from other sources Father Hogan conceived the idea that he could do no greater service to religion or humanity than to induce the poor classes of Catholics to leave the crowded cities and go out and settle on the lands. To carry out this idea he resigned the pastorship of St. Michael's in the summer of 1857 and undertook the founding of a colony in southeast Missouri in

Bishop Hogan summarized his Irish sabbatical to a *K.C. Journal* reporter:
I went directly to County Limerick, my old home. I found few of my old associates there alive. I spent the winter at Connaughton Falls, on the Shannon. It is a wonderfully beautiful spot. Last May I went to the seashore, at the mouth of the Shannon, and have been there ever since. My companions were little children. We romped together on the sand and actually every one wanted to come to America with me.
These experiences awoke memories of his childhood and coming to America. Several years later, Hogan wrote *Fifty Years Ago: A Memoir* but it wasn't published until 1907. Courtesy Springfield-Greene County Library.

> Ripley County. But the colony did not prove a success. Before it had time to form the Civil War came on and rendered its success an impossibility.

The failure of the immigrant colony in southern Missouri obviously had not tarnished Father Hogan's reputation. For sixteen years, Archbishop Peter Richard Kenrick had been impressed by Hogan's commitment and uncommon set of skills. When the young seminary candidate first presented himself to Kenrick, he was handed a Latin book and asked to translate. Later in life Hogan's official correspondence in Latin circulated among priests as models. In his early missionary years, Hogan's fluency in Gaelic was a more useful linguistic skill. Many of the colonists were illiterate and likely spoke native Irish better than English. Having visited outlying parishes in his early days in St. Louis, Kenrick appreciated how proficient Hogan was at frontier travel. The Archbishop knew John Hogan's reluctance to accept a promotion was not due to a lack of qualifications. Kenrick knew Hogan had a large range of ability and he was proven correct.

If reluctant to leave his bucolic mission, John Hogan nevertheless bowed to God and Archbishop Kenrick's will. His administration of the St. Joseph diocese was judged so successful Hogan was in 1880 appointed bishop of the new See of Kansas City, Missouri. For thirteen years he remained Apostolic Administrator of St. Joseph while organizing the larger newly created diocese. The workload took a toll on his health. In a state of near collapse, he was granted a sabbatical and he sailed for Ireland for a thirteen month rest on the Fourth of July, 1894.

There is a ledger book stamped "Return of Bishop Hogan from Ireland" in the archives of the diocese of Kansas City-St. Joseph with neatly cut out and pasted yellowing newspaper clippings. A HERO OF THE CROSS proclaimed the *Kansas City Journal* of August 28, 1895. A special railroad car was sent to Cameron to carry Bishop Hogan and a group of clergy and city dignitaries on the final leg of his journey home. Due to a drawbridge not being down, the train was late. At Union Station, four thousand people waited. Another "three thousand men, armed with flags and torchlights gathered on Broadway, near 10th Street."

> It was 8:25 o'clock when the train ran onto a siding about 100 feet north of the depot. ... One by one the passengers dismounted. As each man stepped upon the platform, he was closely scrutinized by a thousand eager eyes. A glance showed that the first man was not the hero of the hour, and necks were craned to get a look at the next passenger to alight. Finally a man well advanced in years, but with erect figure and eyes that flashed with pleasure as he saw the assembled host, stepped from the train. There was little in his costume of somber black, cut in the conventional clerical style, or in the brown straw hat that was pressed firmly down on a head of nearly snow white hair, to distinguish him from other members of the clergy, but when an exuberant Irishman shouted 'It's the old mon, himself, God bless him,' everyone knew who he meant.

Bystanders "doffed their hats as the Bishop passed and he freely bestowed the pontifical blessing upon them." In a carriage "bedecked with American flags" followed by twenty-three other carriages of dignitaries the procession moved to the cathedral through streets lined with cheering crowds. Those in the parade "all carried torch lights or flags and marched to the music of five bands." Arriving at the Church of the Immaculate Conception, the Bishop made his way to the front between two rows of American flags. Father John J. Glennon, then rector of the cathedral and Hogan's Vicar General, delivered a welcome home speech.

Afterwards Bishop Hogan informally met with friends and reporters in his residence behind the cathedral. He told of boarding the *Britannic* of the White Star Line on the Fourth of July and having a "feeling of loneliness come over me:"

> Think of it! It was the great and only Fourth and there we were, outward bound and not a sign of the Stars and Stripes. ... Why do you know, he said with one of his particular smiles, that some Englishman on board took occasion to sing 'God Save the Queen,' and that upon the Fourth. ... I don't suppose the average American realizes that one thing that has quite an influence in causing Irish immigration is the kind treatment of the poor by people of this country. The English seem to have the idea that the poor should be kicked out of the way whenever they cross their path. This the Irish resent more than anyone realizes. Let me show you how a Briton walks though the streets of an Irish city. They always have a cane. I must

Bishop Hogan went from building an $85.31 log church in the wilderness to constructing a $125,000 pro-cathedral but his fiscal conservatism didn't change. An 1883 newspaper article describing the impressive edifice in Kansas City noted that the interior was not complete yet, but would be "when the Bishop has the funds in hand to meet the bills, as he abhors going in debt ... even as he abhors sin." It would be 1912, more than twenty years later, before the stained glass windows, the final touch, were put in place.

> have a cane, said the Bishop, looking around. Not finding the necessary stick, he reached into the wastebasket, pulled out a piece of foolscap paper, crumpled it into an extremely short walking stick, and swaggered across the floor with a stride that would have made a Piccadilly swell turn green with envy. As he walked he kicked an imaginary beggar from in front of him.

Like many who fled the Famine, John Hogan still had strong feelings about the British domination of Ireland. He and many other immigrants had, after a period of struggle, become successful in the new world. At a banquet given in his honor by the Daughters of Erin a few weeks after his triumphant return, it's unlikely there were any poor Catholic servant girls who cleaned Protestant houses. Nor were there any itinerant railroad laborers among the men

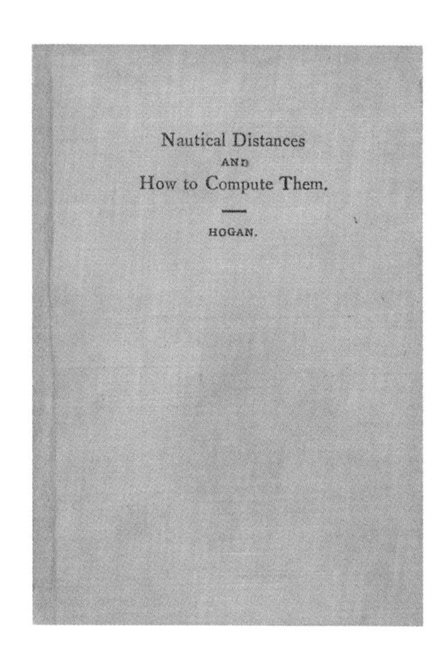

After his return from Ireland in 1894, Hogan's duties kept him in the Kansas City area. His interests in traveling to distant places and in America's role in worldwide political events were undiminished. Prompted by U.S. involvement in the Spanish American War, in 1903, the Rt. Rev. John J. Hogan published a small manual, *Nautical Distances and How to Compute Them*, for school instruction. He dedicated it to President Theodore Roosevelt. Courtesy Kansas City-St. Joseph Diocese Archives.

seated by the ladies of Irish ancestry. Forty years earlier, Father Hogan had feared that "the total separation of these immigrants" would create "a most anomalous condition ... practically debarring them from intermarriage." His colony in the Ozarks was founded as a solution to that problem. Here was a hall of lively evidence that Irish Catholicism had not become an endangered heritage.

The *Kansas City Times* sent a reporter to cover "the royal welcome to his grace. ... On the stage was a handsome stand of colors, the star-spangled banner in the center, the white and yellow flag of the papacy, and the green standard of the Emerald Isle." The New York Count Oysters, Young Turkey, Shrimp, Ham, etc. and fifty assorted cakes made by the Daughters of Erin were "nonetheless toothsome because served by a score or more of pretty women who wore the greenest aprons anyone ever saw." An address in "regular old Gaelic" was followed by a few words from the guest of honor. Hogan spoke of the beauty of Ireland and its continuing poverty that he blamed on British rule. But he was optimistic. "I say that landlordism in Ireland is doomed and home rule is coming." Ex-Mayor Cowherd of Kansas City toasted Hogan with a glass of pure cold water. The Mayor praised Hogan's accomplishments. "Some of us are neither Irishmen nor Catholics and yet we, too, hold you, Bishop, in the highest honor and esteem." Afterward the band struck up "Home Sweet Home" with Mrs. Kate Conway singing the words. "Daniel O'Byrne now stepped forward and presented the bishop with a magnificent floral offering, fully three feet high, of roses, jasmine, heliotrope, and a score of other blooms. It was an Irish harp. Mr. O'Byrne said:

> To you, Reverend Bishop, we present this harp, as one particularly fitted to be its recipient. The Irish priesthood has been a maker as well as a product of Irish character. That aspiration for, and appreciation of the good, the true and the beautiful which the Irish have naturally as a people, has, in a great measure, been preserved to them in the dark days of their adversity by the clergy.

After his long Irish vacation, John Hogan returned reinvigorated. To everyone's surprise the aging bishop now seemed disinclined to retire. This development came as a shock to young Father John Glennon whom Hogan had recommended to be his coadjutor with right of succession.

Nicholas Schneider tells of Glennon's frustration in his *The Life of John Cardinal Glennon*:

> Since Hogan had asked for help everyone expected him to step aside, giving his coadjutor a free field. Glennon certainly presumed it. Not long after his consecration he called at the Bishop's house to offer his services but the older man found new life in his coadjutor's elevation. Though worn out by 44 years of long and arduous labor, 28 of them as bishop, he politely but firmly informed Glennon that he still had adequate vitality and that the young bishop must be prepared to face the uncertainties of life, for he knew an elderly bishop of Limerick who had buried two coadjutors. This remark set the tone for the relationship between the two men during the next seven years as Hogan persistently hampered Glennon in his administration of diocesan affairs. However, their differences were forgotten in later years and when Hogan died in February 1913, Glennon preached his eulogy.

John Joseph Glennon left Kansas City to become coadjutor of St. Louis when Archbishop John Joseph Kain's health failed. Several months later in 1903, Kain died and Glennon succeeded him. For most of their time together, Hogan and Glennon had been close. Hogan had in fact arranged for the future archbishop and cardinal to come to Kansas City from an Irish seminary before he was ordained. It is not known if the two ever discussed Hogan's settlement of immigrants in the hills of southeast Missouri. Interestingly, Glennon founded a settlement for German immigrants only fifty miles from the Irish Wilderness in the lowlands of southeast Missouri in 1905, soon after becoming archbishop.

He created the Colonization Realty Company purchasing twelve thousand acres of fertile but overflow lands to resell to Catholic immigrant farmers. Many descendants of the original German and Dutch settlers still live in the area and celebrate Mass at St. Teresa's church in Glennonville.

John Joseph Hogan caught a cold that developed into pneumonia. He died on February 21, 1913. Archbishop Glennon came from St. Louis to pronounce absolution and read the bishop's instructions for his burial at his funeral. The *Kansas City Post* reported Glennon's words. "Let my casket and grave be simple and of small cost," the Archbishop read, "and let no sermon accompany the last rites. And, indeed, no ceremony is needed," continued Archbishop Glennon. "The souls he saved, the friends he made, the words he spoke, the work he did, the life he led, speak more eloquently than words." The eighty three year old bishop's death and burial were page one news in the *Kansas City Journal* and the *Kansas City Post*.

44 YEARS PRELATE BISHOP HOGAN DIES
In the Priesthood two thirds of his long and useful life
CONSCIOUS NEAR END

BISHOP J.J. HOGAN BURIED
Hundreds Unable To Enter Cathedral Kneel In Snow During High Mass
CORTEGE TWO MILES LONG

J.J. Hogan had always been good copy. Everyone in Kansas City knew him. His habit of taking a streetcar to the end of the line and walking back five or six miles was noted in the coverage of his death. The bishop had always been available for interviews and gave concise, knowledgeable quotes on current affairs. On his deathbed, *The Kansas City Star* reported, "He expressed slight regret that he would not be able to complete his studies of the Near East that he might know all the causes and conditions leading up to the present struggle there." In a follow up article, the *Star* revealed Hogan's will. Explaining that in spite of the custom in the Catholic Church for all the property in the diocese to be held in the bishop's name, Hogan died poor. His $2,500 life insurance policy was distributed to charity. His library of two thousand books he left to his coadjutor and successor, Bishop Thomas Lillis. "After the funeral expenses are paid there won't be enough of Bishop Hogan's private money left to make a pauper rich," Father O'Reilly said. And of course the newspapers revisited the exceptional stories of his days as a pioneer priest. Heroes of the frontier were mostly Scotch-Irish adventurers, not Irish Catholic priests.

Near the end of *On the Mission on Missouri* is a passage that goes to the heart of John Hogan's reluctance to leave his country mission to become a city prelate. His love of nature and his vision of its harmonious utilization are intertwined:

> The threatened illness brought on by exposure and fatigue

Silver anniversary cabinet card of Bishop Hogan 1893. Though the unostentatious Hogan attempted to limit the September, 1893 celebration of his twenty-fifth year as a bishop, several thousand called at the episcopal residence following a modest ceremony at the Cathedral. Among his well-wishers were his brother, P. J. Hogan of Baltimore; his nephews, Father Hogan and Brother Justus Hogan; cousin, Sister Mary Bernard; and niece, Sister Clara Joseph. The Irish Hogans were a large clan and many, like John Joseph, had immigrated to America and many served the Church.

in the month of January having entirely passed away, I was soon out again, revisiting the missions of Bethany, Eagleville, Akron and Princeton, where, as before, I said Mass, heard confessions, gave instructions, administered baptism, and afforded opportunity to the faithful to comply fully with their Christian duties. Later on in the spring, or rather in the month of May, towards the end of the Paschal Time, I set out to complete the missionary journey, which the inclement weather of January had compelled me to temporarily abandon. But how different now from stormy midwinter were the beautiful days of spring. Vegetation had already come on apace. The elder, hazel, elm, and the silver maple were in full vigor of life. The willow, gooseberry, and rose bushes had shaken off their icy fringes, and were bursting their petals into full leaf and blossom. The peach, apple and pear trees, gaily dressed in exuberant bloom, were scattering over the ground their

> superabundant floral wealth that filled the air with sweetest fragrance. Everywhere the wild plum and cherry, and the red-bud and flowering locust, had spread out their bright many colored banners, and their drapery of magnificence and glory.
>
> Far and near and all around, and away in the remotest distances of the horizon, the endless prairie in its bright mantle of green, dotted with turretted islands of leafy forest, and traversed by winding streams fringed with waving willows and drooping elms, basked and glowed in the warm sunshine that gave all nature life. Where now were the piercing winds, the frozen icy bands, and the pelting snow flakes of winter? The ploughman, too, was abroad, with gladness in his steps, following his merry horses, as they rushed the ploughshare through the mellow lea. It was no wonder that the joyousness of his resonant voice, as he talked and sang to his team, outvied the little birds of the forest, that sang on the bushes and on the tree-tops around him; for in his gladsome heart, he foresaw the teeming granaries and the fruitful harvests, that were to reward his labors.
>
> O beautiful prairies of Missouri, so often and for so many years the joy of my heart, well I have said in my younger days, when first I heard of your transcendent loveliness, and when friends would tempt my youthful feet to other climes; O no, leave me my joy; Missouri's my home; I love her for her woods and prairies; amid these let my grave be made; under the bending boughs of her forests I long to die.

But "under the bending boughs of her forests" he did not die. Nor was he buried on the lone prairie. He, like most Irish immigrants, probably even many of the survivors of the colony, ended up in the city. The Potato Famine migration coincided with the growth of industrialization and urbanization and the decline of meaningful opportunities to settle on cheap undeveloped land. By Hogan's death in 1913, there were few unplowed prairies or uncut forests in Missouri. Even in 1859, the best land had been taken.

The Irish contribution to American urban life is well documented. Not a few Irish immigrants were or—as in Hogan's case—became priests. Some rose in the ranks of the Catholic Church and had distinguished careers. Indeed, the Irish influence came to dominate American Catholicism. The lives of many Irish-born prelates are commemorated

John Joseph Hogan has become part of Missouri folklore. Here, a re-enactor plays Father Hogan on horseback in a parade that opened Cameron's 1955 centennial celebration. The pioneer priest was also a player in a pageant for six nights at the high school stadium. Father Hogan built Cameron's first church in 1867. Photo courtesy Kansas City-St. Joseph Diocese Archives.

by fine tombstones in well kept cemeteries. Bishop John Joseph Hogan's granite headstone is on a hill overlooking Kansas City in St. Mary's cemetery. As well as good works, his legacy includes a readable text of his experiences shaping the new world and being shaped by it. But for the disruptions of the War Between the States, the authors of this book believe Hogan's settlement would have succeeded modestly, as Hogan anticipated. His brave but failed colony of poor Irish in the Ozark wilderness became legend, a small but durable marker of the human aspiration to prosper through faith and freedom.

RIGHT REV. JOHN JOSEPH HOGAN, D.D.,

FIRST BISHOP OF KANSAS CITY AND FIRST BISHOP OF ST. JOSEPH'S.

JOHN JOSEPH HOGAN was born in the parish of Bruff, County and Diocese of Limerick, Ireland, on May 10, 1829. His first studies at the age of five were at the village school of the Holy Cross and then at his father's house under a private teacher of Latin and Greek. When eighteen years old, already aspiring to the priesthood, he came to St. Louis and entered the Theological Seminary of the Diocese and was ordained a priest in April, 1852. His studies had been thorough from the beginning. He commenced his missionary career at Old Mines, and next as pastor at Potosi, showing in both places an aptitude for missionary labor. In 1854 he became an assistant at St. John's Church, in St. Louis, and at the same time chaplain to the Male Orphan Asylum and spiritual director and confessor to the Sisters. His next work was to organize the new parish of St. Michael; he erected the church and built parochial schools. He now showed the true apostolic spirit in leaving the parish, where he had created all, for a remote, vast and unprovided missionary field, Northwest Missouri, which had neither pastor nor church, and he founded the missions at Martinsburg, Mexico, Sturgeon, Allen (now called Moberly), Macon City, Brookfield, Chillicothe and Cameron. After having energetically and zealously founded the missions of Northwest Missouri, he went to the South and commenced a similar work on the State border near Arkansas. Here, however, the ravages of civil war prevented all his noble efforts. On March 3, 1868, the Holy See erected the See of St. Joseph's, containing all that part of Missouri lying between the St. Louis and Charitan Rivers. Father Hogan was appointed its Bishop and he was consecrated by Most Rev. P. R. Kenrick at St. Louis on September 13, 1868. The new Diocese, embracing parts of his former missions, contained then nine priests, eleven churches and fourteen thousand Catholics. Schools for boys were already conducted by the Brothers of the Christian Schools, and for girls by the Ladies of the Sacred Heart. The Benedictines and Franciscans were received, as also the Benedictine Sisters, the Sisters of St. Joseph and of the Perpetual Adoration. Schools, churches and institutions sprang up on all sides. In 1880, in September, the See of Kansas City was erected, containing that part of Missouri south of the Missouri and west of Moniteau, Miller, Camden, Laclede, Wright, Douglas and Ozark counties. Bishop Hogan was appointed its first Bishop and administrator of St. Joseph's. The Redemptorists came and made Kansas City the centre of their western missions. The Little Sisters of the Poor opened a home for the aged. Progress was made on all sides. The two Dioceses now possess sixty-three priests, forty-four churches, twenty-eight stations and nine chapels, one college, eight academies, one orphan asylum, four hospitals, one Magdalene asylum, one industrial home for girls, a home for the aged, nearly three thousand children attending parochial schools, and a Catholic population of twenty-eight thousand five hundred. Kansas City contains the Novitiate of the Redemptorists.

FILI HOMINIS
PVTAS NE OSSA ISTA
REVIVISCENT

(Opposite) Hogan's career as summarized in the 1889 *Illustrated History of The Catholic Church in the United States*. It briefly acknowledges the failed Irish colony in the Ozarks as well as his current successes.

IHS

Hic tumulantur ossa et
Cineres Joannis Josephi
Hogan Proto- Episcopi Kan=.
san opolitani.
Natus A.D 1829. Vixit an=
nos 8---, in Episcopatu 4---
Orate pro eo.

(Right) Hogan's final resting place is in the "clergy lot where my brother priests are buried" in St. Mary's Cemetery on a hill with a distant view of downtown Kansas City. His handwritten epitaph was published in the *Kansas City Star*.
Here are buried the bones and ashes of John Joseph Hogan, first Bishop of Kansas City. Born 1829 A.D. lived 8..., years as Bishop 4....
Pray for him.

BIBLIOGRAPHY

An expanded list of references for the Irish Wilderness and Bishop John Joseph Hogan can be found in *On the Mission in Missouri* & *Fifty Years Ago: A Memoir*, also published by Lens & Pen Press.

Books

Crawford, Mike. *Father Hogan's 1859 Irish Wilderness Settlement.* Doniphan, Missouri: Printed by the Prospect-News, ND.

Hogan, Rev. John J.. *Fifty Years Ago: A Memoir.* Kansas City: Franklin Hudson Publishing Co., 1907.

—. *On the Mission in Missouri: 1857-1868.* Kansas City: John A. Heilmann, 1892.

Marra, Dorothy Brandt, and Rev. Michael Coleman. *This Far by Faith. I & II*, Marceline, Missouri: Diocese of Kansas City-St. Joseph, 1992

O'Hanlon, John. *Reverend John O'Hanlon's The Irish Immigrant's Guide for the United States.* Edward J. Maguire. New York: Arno Press, 1976.

—. *Life and Scenery in Missouri.* Dublin: James Duffy and Co., 1890.

Ponder, Jerry. *A History of the 15th Missouri Cavalry Regiment CSA.* Doniphan: Ponder Books, 1994.

Rothsteiner, John. *History of the Archdiocese of St. Louis.* First ed. *I & II*, Blackwell Wielandy, Inc, 1928.

Schneider, Nicholas. *The Life of John Cardinal Glennon.* Liguori, Missouri: Liguori Publications, 1971.

Simpson, Lewis A.W. *Oregon County's Three Flags.* Keith Johnson. Thayer, Missouri: Thayer News, 1971.

History & Families Ripley County, Missouri. Paducah, Kentucky: Turner Publishing Co., Revised, Third Printing, 2003.

Newspapers, Magazines and Journals

Allen, Edgar. "Current River - Descendant of Springs." *The Missouri Conservationist*, July, 1948, 1-3.

Cullimore, Dan. Twelve part series on the history of the Irish Wilderness. *St. Louis Post-Dispatch*, December 1951 and January 1952.

Hammar, Conrad H. "Institutional Aspects of Ozark Decline." *Journal of Forestry* 33, no. 10 (1935): 843-850.

Saults, Dan, and Don Wooldridge. "The Irish Wilderness." *The Missouri Conservationist*, August, 1951, 11-15.

"Story of a Great Enterprise." *American Lumberman*, May 9, 1903, 43-90.

Web-based Sources

Flader, Susan. "Sand County Anniversary." May, 1999. *Missouri Conservationist Online.* mdc.mo.gov/conmag (accessed 10/24/2007).

Suttle, Gary. "Aldo Leopold." home.utm.net/pan/leopold.html (accessed 10/21/2007).